I Kiss Your Little Hand
Madame . . .
and more disasters abroad

Also by COLIN REID

Do You Take This Woman: and more disasters
Life with My Wife: and other disasters

I kiss your little hand, madame...

AND MORE DISASTERS ABROAD

COLIN REID

Drawings by
Colin Reid, Jnr.

CRESSRELLES
Publishing Company Limited

First published in 1977 by
Cressrelles Publishing Company Limited
Kestrels House, Peppard Common, Oxfordshire

ISBN 0 85956 017 1

Printed in Great Britain by
Biddles Ltd., Guildford, Surrey

PUBLISHER'S NOTE

Colin Reid needs no introduction to the millions of readers who have followed his humorous columns in the *Daily Mail*, *Reveille* and various magazines. He is the father of three children and two books *Do You Take This Woman? . . . and more Disasters* and *Life With My Wife . . . and other Disasters* which chronicle his failed campaigns in the sex war and the eyeball-to-eyeball confrontations of parenthood.

Involved in the events he looks back on here - a family holiday abroad - were his wife, known to his newspaper readers as the Chief Fairy (the nickname stuck after she was once discovered paying inflationary prices for newly-tugged milk teeth under their five-year-old's pillow); also his two younger children, Gavin, then aged 10, and Christine, 14.

It all happened in the Spring of '72, when the pound rode high against the peseta and the franc, God was in His Heaven and all was nearly right with the world. Oh, happy days! Oh, sweet nostalgia!

As with the author's last book, his eldest son, Colin jnr., now an artist and married, has entered into the spirit of the family's foreign fling by doing the illustrations and book jacket.

Contents

1 Something Exciting . . .

It was Gavin's idea. 'Dad,' he said, 'do you think we could do something really exciting this Easter?'

'Like what?' I said guardedly. Usually his notion of doing something exciting involves me in no end of trouble and expense. At that moment I had no wish to face either. I was lying flat on my back on my Saturday couch trying to dismiss from my mind the fact that not only were the spring flowers blooming, tra-la, but so were the spring weeds and lawn, tra-la, and soon I would have to do something about it.

I glanced at him for amplification of this 'something exciting' but he'd suddenly gone quiet, lost in his 11-minus thoughts. He was staring out of the garden window at a rainbow struggling through another April shower. For most of the morning he had been wandering about listlessly blowing the funeral march on his melodica - a tune that certainly reflected the mood of bored restlessness which seemed to have settled on the household, but did nothing for the cat's spirits. As the mournful notes rang out, Smokey's head and whiskers had slumped lower between her paws in front of the fire. Her whole expression suggested, 'What a tune for Spring!'

Nor was it improved by the muffled lament of a love song being strummed on a guitar upstairs by Christine beneath the pop idol gallery that lines her bedroom wall. Still, spring's a tough time for 14-year-olds, too.

But now the funeral march had stopped, for which Smokey at least was grateful. She stretched out her paws, yawned mightily and began to wash herself.

Gavin turned from the window. 'Couldn't we go abroad?' he said urgently. It was as though he'd seen something at the end of the rainbow.

'Abroad?'

'Yes, I've never been abroad. Not ever. Not in my whole life.'

He made it sound a terrible denial for a father to be guilty of, as though I'd failed to give him any names at birth.

'You'll be going to Ireland again in the summer holidays,' I countered. 'That's abroad. That's another country.'

'I don't mean *that*,' he said witheringly, as though he were dealing with a blockhead. 'I mean *really* abroad like Spain or France or places like that. All the other children at school are always going to those places, where they have different languages and money and things. They're always writing about them when we have to do our holiday essays at the start of term. And all *I* can write about is silly old Ireland all the time. I keep having to put the same old stuff down every term.'

'But you always say you love Ireland. You ask to go back every year,' I said.

'I know I do, but I want to go somewhere *different* abroad so

I can write about it. I still want to go to Ireland in the summer, but I'm talking about now, this Easter. If we went to Spain or France I could write about that, couldn't I?'

So! I'm to provide the lad with two holidays - one for fun and one to write about in his school essays, just because he's written out on the subject of Ireland! As if I didn't have enough trouble as legman and research assistant in his classroom projects.

'What about the cost? My name's Reid, not Rockefeller.'

'Who's he?'

'Never mind. Do you know how much it costs to get a car across the Channel and stay in those French hotels?'

'How would I know!' he exploded. 'That's what I mean, I've never been!'

I began to wish he'd stuck to his funeral march.

'Well, you can take it from me it costs a bomb,' I muttered, turning over on the sofa. 'Ask your mother.'

He turned to address his mother, then decided it was probably a waste of breath. At that moment she was in a kind of trance in her favourite rocker, oblivious, it seemed, to everything. She was on her spring diet and had just spent the last ten minutes torturing herself with multi-coloured dishes and recipes in a woman's magazine. While the rest of the family had lunched well on sausages and chips, she had nibbled at what looked like two nuts and a lettuce leaf, which is hardly enough to keep a small pixie on, let alone a Chief Fairy.

The last we had heard from her was a groan of 'Oh, God!' as her eyes glazed over at a coloured spread of forbidden flans. She slumped back in her rocker, closing her eyes in a coma of frustration.

Gavin turned back to me. 'It's all right for you lot - you and mum and even Christine. You've all been abroad before I was born. But I haven't. You all know what it's like to live there and talk their language and eat their food and all that sort of thing. But I can't write a *thing* about it!'

At the word 'food' the Chief Fairy stiffened and emerged from her coma.

It was obvious that little of the preceding conversation had penetrated her calorie-starved grey cells, so I gave a quick run-down on how the package-tour essayists of the first form were pressurising our budding Montaigne. He had no paella to write about or frogs' legs or *vin du pays* because he'd never been to the Continent.

There was a long silence in which it dawned on me - too late - that I had chosen the wrong accent to stress. I should have said that our son was anxious to repair his lack of knowledge on French narrow-gauge railways or the deciduous tree content of the Dordogne. Fool that I was I mentioned food. Her eyes were already misting.

'Actually, I suppose he's right really,' she said, her rocker beginning to sway back and forth. 'We never have taken him abroad. It's something he's missed.' Her gaze became fixed on some dream hanging over the garden. 'Yes, it might be a good idea to show him a bit of France or Spain, or somewhere like that. In fact, it could be quite exciting for all of us.'

Her rocker was quickening its pace and you didn't need to be a psychologist to realise that what was exciting was the prospect of crashing off her diet and onto some of those French dishes. All she needed was the excuse.

'There you are!' said Gavin, visibly delighted at finding an ally in his mother. 'Mum's all for it, see!'

Not only was he delighted, he was amazed. As far as he is concerned her usual game is to stop him doing anything that sounds exciting or adventurous.

I mentioned the cost again, but the Chief Fairy's rocker was in a swinging groove of anticipation. 'I'm sure if we were careful and stayed at cheap places it wouldn't be too expensive,' she said enthusiastically. 'The thing to do each night would be to take one of those large family rooms with two double beds, because the French charge by the room. Then in the mornings we could just have coffee and croissants.' She moistened her lips. 'They do delicious coffee and croissants, Gavin, you'd love them.'

Gavin's eyebrows went up - he couldn't care less about coffee and croissants, but he wasn't going to argue.

'And at lunch-time we could picnic with our own wine and

cheese and pate and French bread which we could buy very cheaply in the shops. Their pate is delicious! Then at night' - her rocker was reaching a sinful crescendo - 'at night we could have a really slap-up French meal in a proper restaurant. Oh, their food is gorgeous, honestly, absolutely gorgeous!' she gulped.

At last the truth was out. There was a moment's silence for readjusting sights. Even Gavin recognised the urges that had presented him with an ally in his mother. He can't stand fancy food - chicken, chips and Coke is as fancy as he wants to get, but he didn't intend to stare a gift horse in its yearning mouth.

'Smashing!' he said.

'Here, hang about -' I began.

'No, no, it's agreed, two-to-one!' he cut in excitedly. 'We're all going abroad! And Christine will make it three-to-one, I'll bet.' Before I could stop him he ran out of the room and shouted upstairs, 'Christine! Christine! Do you want to go abroad?'

The guitar music stopped. Christine came down, puzzled. 'Go abroad? What do you mean? When?'

'This Easter! Next week! Do you? Go on, make it three-to-one! We all want to go except Dad.' And why worry about him? He's only paying the bills.

Christine hesitated. 'Whereabouts abroad?' But Gavin had already learned the lesson, from his mother's enthusiasm, that everybody has a price. In his mother's case he had stumbled on it fortuitously - mouth-watering French calories.

'We're going to France,' he said enthusiastically. 'Isn't that where they pinch all the girls' bottoms? Very sexy! You'd love it, Christine!' He began to fall about, not only at his own wit but at the thought of having brought off another coup.

'Don't be ridiculous!' she retorted. 'That's Italy where they do that and it isn't sexy at all. It's offensive.'

'Oh.' His face fell. For a moment I thought I'd found an ally. But the hope was short-lived. Oh, fickle women! Just when you think they're on your side they're not on your side at all.

'They don't pinch bottoms in France,' she said. 'They don't need to.' Her eyes were misting over, just like her mother's but for different reasons. She gazed out of the garden window. 'You only have to listen to their love songs to know that the French really know how to treat a woman,' she murmured.

I suddenly recalled that she was between loves, her last romance with a gangly and slightly spotty 16-year-old having ended abruptly for reasons revealed only to her diary. Perhaps he had found another, perhaps he had fallen short of her romantic dream in some way, perhaps . . . but who knows what goes on in the mind of a teenage girl, except maybe another teenage girl? All I know is that sometimes, when things are going very well or very badly, she can lie for hours in her bedroom pouring out all the pangs into the pages of her diary. Which, of course, I never see.

Anyway, I was clearly beaten and democratically, three-to-one. Or rather three-to-two if you count Smokey on my side. Her ears had pricked up instinctively at the general commotion and the foreign names being bandied about. You can't fool a cat. She knew that if there was going to be an additional holiday it meant her for the cats' home for another fortnight. She hates the cats' home. She looked at me, miaowed loudly and slunk towards the door.

'Well, you hadn't actually planned anything for this Easter, had you?' the Chief Fairy said - a bit late in the day, I thought.

'Yes,' I said, 'I was going to mow the lawn.'

That did it. 'Hooray, we're going abroad!' Gavin shouted, and as a salute to the venture he grabbed his melodica and began to march round the room playing '*Allons Enfants de la Patrie* . . .'

Well, I thought, perhaps the prospect of the open French roads, French cooking and unplanned stops at little rural inns might not be so bad after all. I'm a great believer in the philosophy that if you've got to have it you might as well relax and enjoy it, and already a holiday plan was forming in my mind.

What we could do was take the car ferry from Southampton to Cherbourg, then head down through Brittany, across Western

France to the Dordogne, on through the Spanish border and, if we were still in one piece, the Costa Brava. That should give the lad something to write about.

The idea of visiting Brittany had taken hold in my mind almost from the moment that Smokey and I had been outvoted by the holiday committee. Indeed, it had more than taken hold, it was now filling me with a mixture of excitement and nostalgic yearning. As a boy of 12 I had been taken on my own first visit to France on a family holiday and I remembered it vividly.

I had gone there with my parents, my two brothers and baby sister and we had sailed from Southampton to St. Malo, then by the tiny ferry to Dinard across the bay. It had been a marvellous, idyllic holiday in a long, hot summer just before the war, but it was to be the last holiday we were to spend together. The war came, the family broke up and grew up, and soon all the childhood days were gone.

Though I had never been back to Dinard since that summer I remembered so much of it clearly - the bay of soft, golden sand, warm Gulf Stream waters that you could swim and play in all day, the old walled city of St. Malo, with its winding, cobbled streets and, remarkably after all these years, even the little family hotel where we had stayed. I couldn't remember its name, but I knew exactly where I would find it - looking out across the bay near the ferry landing point. If, of course, it was still there.

I mentioned my plan to the family. 'It sounds great,' said Christine. 'Can I take my guitar?'

'Sure.'

'And can I take my melodica?' Gavin said quickly.

'Bring the whole orchestra. If we run out of money I can always put you both on the streets busking.'

'Whoopee!' said Gavin. 'This time next week we'll be in France!' He began to leap up and down on my sofa.

'And I'll keep on my diet till we get there,' the Chief Fairy announced firmly, suddenly standing up and looking at herself sideways in the mirror. 'Then I can splurge!'

The mood was definitely buoyant. It was also, for me, somewhat nerve-jarring and noisy on the sofa and I suddenly found myself warming to a secret hope. Perhaps this Continental journey might do for my Euro-family what Britain's entry into the Common Market had so far failed to do, infect them with some of that loving and respectful subservience to the head of the house that seems to characterise the French family.

You know the sort of thing I mean. Apart from what I've seen at first hand, I've been reading about it since I was knee-high to my first French master. Remember the Duval family and the Dupont family in those early French primers? Lovely families - always being respectful to *Papa*, going for walks *dans le parc* and shopping *dans le marché*. And how pleased they all were to see father come home from his day's *travail*.

'*Papa est arrive. Comment allez-vous, Papa?*' Always very concerned about his health and quite right, too. None of that British blundering past him, whooping war cries in his ear. And Madame, too - none of that 'You're late, what kept you?' Not at all.

As I remember it, the greeting went something like '*Bonsoir, mon cheri! Tu seras content de savoir que j'ai coupé la pelouse et lavé la voiture pendant ton absence!*' (For those who have not followed their Dubonnet lessons - 'Good evening, my love! You will be happy to know that I have cut the lawn and washed the car during your absence!)

If some of this attentive, respectful subservience could rub off during our French travels I would count the cost well worth it.

I would have felt more uplifted than I did but, at that moment, I caught sight of Smokey staring at me from the doorway. Sometimes I feel that a strange telepathy exists between us, and a quick flush of goosepimples rose on my neck.

What she seemed to be saying in her clairvoyant way was: 'Don't blame *me* for what's going to happen . . .'

2 'Are We Nearly There, Dad?'

With only a few days to prepare for the journey the sense of urgency and excitement mounted higher each morning. There were ferry bookings to make, Green Card insurance to apply for, the car to service for the 2,000-mile tour we were planning, continental road maps to supply ourselves with, as well as francs and pesetas - and, oh yes, a tent in case of emergency.

Gavin's eyes lit up at that when he saw me pulling it out of the garage clutter. 'Great!' he said. 'Camping, too!' But I quickly disabused him of the idea. That, I said, was only in case of some disaster. My Scouting life is long gone and I'm one for the pleasures of a comfortable bed and waiter-served breakfast.

For her own part the Chief Fairy had launched into a flurry of washing, cleaning, ironing and shopping for last-minute needs. Each morning she would hound us round the house with 'Don't wear that! You'll need that clean for the holiday, wear your old stuff!'

This happens every holiday. Several days before we depart I am seen around my favourite haunts dressed as though I've just been kitted out by a kindly stallholder at a jumble sale. My friends don't actually start dipping their hands into their pockets for the price of a meal, but it's not far from it.

'Is that really old Colin? Let himself go a bit, hasn't he?' they mutter. Go? I'm going on holiday, that's all, but my wife wants to keep the good stuff clean. All of it.

One night Gavin came pounding downstairs with the plaintive

cry, 'I can't wear these old pyjamas! The buttons are off and there's a hole in the trousers and they're too short!'

He stood there with his sleeves several inches short of his wrists, his pyjama bottoms half way up his calf, and his buttonless jacket flapping open. All good clean stuff, but he looked pretty forlorn, I must say.

'My goodness,' said his mother, delighted and surprised, 'look how he's growing! He's only had those a year.'

'Never mind how I'm growing!' he retorted hotly. 'I can't wear these old things! Suppose somebody sees me - look at me!'

'Nobody's going to see you, don't be ridiculous, she said, but despite herself she started smiling.

'There you are, you're laughing!'

'No, I'm not,' she said, laughing. 'Look, it's only for two days, I'm keeping your two best pairs to pack for France.'

Sitting there in my own tramp's gear and frayed shirt cuffs, I was deeply aware of a fellow-feeling for the lad, but then the ridiculousness of this pre-holiday wardrobe conservation programme and the sight of the young, irate face poking out of the shrivelled pyjamas was too much for me and I yielded to my emotions.

'There! Dad's laughing, too! That does it, I'm definitely not wearing them!' he said angrily. So his mother conceded. 'All right,' she said, still laughing, 'we'll throw them out.'

By the fifth day - we were to depart the following morning - all that remained was the actual packing and the cat to park in the cattery. Oh, how easily both items roll off the tongue.

It never ceases to surprise my friends that I do the packing for the family. They look at me as though I've sprouted a second nose. 'Oh? Not your wife? How interesting,' they say politely, but clearly thinking, 'What sort of a nutcase have we here? A husband who does the *packing?*'

I've had the job ever since my honeymoon. Where I went wrong, apparently, was to offer a small criticism of the way my wife had packed her suitcase. It was a mild enough observation really, just something to jolly the bedroom conversation along, but she was on it like a flash, and I've been the family suitcase packer ever since. I received much pre-honeymoon advice but nobody mentioned a word about suitcases. Not a word.

In the early years it was fairly easy. The family was young and uncritical then, and it was no problem to throw in a few bibs and bonnets on top of our holiday gear and shut the cases. The Chief Fairy was another matter. She'd come to me with a list as long as your arm. 'Just a few things I'll probably need on holiday,' she'd say and start dumping the stuff on the bed, draping it round the room, hanging it from picture rails until you could hardly move - or even *see* because of the light being blocked by the dresses hanging from curtain rails. That's when the whittling had to start.

'What I have here,' I'd say, 'are three suitcases. What you've got there is enough to fill the hold of the Queen Elizabeth. Take that list away and cut it in half.'

'But I *need* it!' she'd plead. 'All of it!'

At least then I had only one rebel to handle. Now they can all write lists, and on the fifth day they brought them to me - with all their worldly goods.

Into the packing centre - our bedroom - came Christine, carrying her first armful and her list. She'd learned well from her mother. There were 62 items on it, starting with four pairs of platform soled shoes and ten pairs of jeans. She was closely followed by Gavin waving a list that started, 'Roler skates, boomerang, kyte . . .' but almost nothing to wear.

Near-revolution followed as I ordered them to decimate the lists. 'But I *need* it all!' they moaned.

'Look,' I said, 'we're going on a fortnight's holiday, not emigrating!'

Just when I felt that I'd managed to introduce some sanity into the operation, in came their mother with her own first armful of plunder from the airing cupboard. Then she turned to raid her wardrobe. I watched amazed as the mountain piled up.

'For heaven's sake I'll never get it all in!' I said.

'What?' she frowned at the Everest of clothes on the bed, topped by a yellow bikini, then almost in agony removed a small silk scarf, followed - more agonisingly - by a cardigan.

'Oh, big deal! Look, half that pile will have to go. You don't need all those dresses and suits!'

She looked aghast. 'But I do!'

Only then did I discover why. She was taking two sizes of everything - one set to fit her figure now, and the other to grow into on holiday.

'Okay, okay,' I sighed, 'I'd been hoping to do without it but I suppose I'd better fit the roof rack.'

'Oh, good,' she said and promptly put the scarf and cardigan back on top of the pile.

At last only Smokey remained to be packed - off to the cats' home. Needless to say, she'd vanished. She knew D-Day had come, with all the bustling, shouting and packing. Her instinct told her what always followed that commotion.

Every holiday eve you'll find me on my hands and knees, looking under beds, in cupboards, under the stairs, giving it the phoney spiel, 'Here, Smokey, nice Smokey, come and see what I've got for you!' Which doesn't fool her one bit.

After searching the house I eventually found her curled up in the darkest corner beneath Gavin's bed. She miaowed plaintively as I grabbed her and thrust her into the laundry basket. She hates the laundry basket. She shrinks from it like a Belsen death wagon but it's the only safe way of transporting her to the cattery. Once outside and free, she'd never stop running.

Nobody else volunteers for the job of cat-napping, of course, The family vanish when this job comes up, yet they always reappear as I'm carrying the thing to the car while it's howling it's head off. 'Oh, poor Smokey,' they say and glare malevolently at me. I feel like the public executioner. It does nothing for my relationship with Smokey either. It usually takes weeks after the holiday before we are back on a friendly, trusting footing again.

Next morning all was excitement, bustle and confusion.

'For heaven's sake, leave the carpet, we'll never get out!'

'I'm just giving it a quick run-over with the vacuum, I shan't be a minute.'

'Who's going to see it? We won't be here!'

'*Somebody,*' she replied evenly, 'could be drying the breakfast dishes while I'm doing this.'

Of all domestic upheavals there's nothing to touch that troop movement on the morning of a family holiday, and for some mad reason known only to herself she always insists on carefully vacuuming the house for the burglars. I think she imagines they'll come in only to run their fingers critically over the dust and shake their heads - 'Cor, look at this lot, Bert - wouldn't rob this place!'

But at last we were ready. The cries of 'Where's my this and where's my that,' had subsided, last-minute things were stuffed into the car, bladders synchronised (for a very good reason I always insist on it) and the holiday countdown ticked up its final seconds. Immersion off, gas off, blast off - we're off! Hooray!

Five minutes later we were back.

I was nearly propelled through the car roof at the shriek in my left ear, 'The milkman! I forgot to leave a note for the milkman!'

When my nerve ends stopped jangling, I turned the car round and returned to the house. She went inside and wrote the note. 'Sorry,' she said when she returned. 'But I'd hate to come back to 28 pints of milk on the doorstep.'

'Is that the lot then?' I said. 'Right - at last we're off. Look out, France, here we come!'

'Are we nearly there, dad?'

'Five miles down the road and are we nearly there, dad!

'No! Of course we're not nearly there and don't start that already. We're nowhere near there!'

'How much farther is it, then?'

'Look - for heaven's sake we've just started! It's 85 miles to Southampton for a start, *then* we've got to board the ferry, *then* it'll take five hours to sail to Cherbourg, *then* we've got to drive to our first hotel, *then* we'll be there. All right? So just settle down, will you? There's miles and miles to go.'

He was silent for a minute, but it was too good to last. 'I think I'm going to be sick, dad - dad I'm *gonnabesick!*'

'Sit on some newspaper.'

'I *am* sitting on some newspaper and it's not helping.'

His mother turned to look at him in the back seat. 'I think you'd better stop the car, dear. He looks awfully pale.'

We stopped. The boy climbed out and stared mournfully into a ditch. I stared mournfully at my watch. 'If he's going to be car-sick every five miles, Lord knows how we're ever going to travel 2,000,' I said. 'As for writing about it, he's never going to see any of it - his head's going to be between his knees all the time.'

'It's all those crisps he was eating before we left,' said Christine.

'Let's hope the French don't sell them then,' I muttered.

'But they do!' she said. 'They call them *les chips!*'

'Let's try to keep the news from him shall we?' I said and looked out of the window again. He was bending greenly over the ditch. A wind was springing up, ruffling his hair. I turned the car radio on and glanced at the grey clouds skudding across the sky. It didn't look too good for the crossing and I was glad I'd taken the precaution of booking a hotel room not too far from our arrival point. On the advice of a travel-writer friend I had made reservations for our first night at a family hotel on the coast at Carteret, a small resort. The next day we could motor leisurely down to Brittany - if we ever got to France at all, that is. The present stop was the umpteenth unscheduled diversion of the morning.

'Hurry up, Gavin!' I called out.

'Leave him alone,' his mother said, 'he'll be all right in a minute. It isn't carsickness, it's just excitement.'

After a while he returned to the car, his face showing more colour. He said he felt better and how much farther was it?

'Did you manage to be sick?' his mother asked. He shook his head slowly, his eyes dully on the road ahead. 'You'd feel better if you could be,' she said.

'Don't worry, he'll get plenty of opportunity,' I said, turning up the radio. 'We'll all get plenty of opportunity - listen to that!'

The weather forecast was on. 'There's a force 9 gale blowing in the Channel.'

'A force 9 gale?' said Gavin, emerging suddenly from his depression. He leaned forward. 'You mean we'll be sailing in a storm at sea?'

'Yes,' I said.

'Great!' He'd seen it all in TV sea dramas, decks awash and oil-skinned helmsmen shouting up the rigging. 'Fantastic!' The colour was flooding back into his cheeks. But it was draining rapidly from the Chief Fairy's.

'Oh, God!' she groaned.

3 'Anyone for Lunch?'

Truly it has been said of seasickness that for the first half hour you are afraid you're going to die and the next half hour you are afraid you're *not* going to die.

The weather forecaster had got it absolutely right. Four hours later, aboard the cross-Channel ferry, we were plunging into the eye-teeth of a sou'wester. The ship rose and fell in a juddering, see-saw motion as gale-lashed waves crashed against the ferry bows, spraying spume high over the fo'csle.

Inside the ship those passengers not swaying in their seats were reeling round the decks and lounges, white-faced and wild-eyed, clutching their mouths and searching for the loos. Not a soul was queueing outside the restaurant for lunch.

'O-o-oh!' the Chief Fairy moaned for the umpteenth time. She lay slumped in a corner seat in the after-lounge, bleakly hypnotised by an empty Coke tin rolling backwards and forwards across the table in front of her. Beside her, Christine looked no better. Only Gavin, remarkably and despite my earlier prediction, seemed totally unaffected by the ship's motion.

Indeed from the moment we had boarded the ferry he'd been alive with excitement and at once set off to explore it from stem to stern, examining the lifeboats and all the nautical equipment.

By a happy coincidence the ship's Chief Purser turned out to be an old friend from my Navy days, and he obtained permission for us all to visit the bridge and see the captain take the ship out of harbour.

'Fantastic!' said Gavin - though he and I were the only ones to accept the invitation. Mental and physical deterioration had already set in with the other two, which was more due to fear than fact. We were then only 50 yards from the quayside and hardly a tremor had been felt through the ship.

'You two go, we'll stay here,' moaned the Chief Fairy.

'You mean you don't want to see the bridge and the captain and the wheel and everything?' he said amazed. How could anybody turn down such a fantastic opportunity like that he wanted to know? 'Very easily,' his mother muttered.

So up to the bridge the two of us went. Of course it was nothing like the sailing ships he'd seen on TV. There were no men in oilskins leaning into gales, spinning enormous wheels and shouting up the rigging. In fact, there was no rigging at all, the bridge was enclosed, the captain murmured his instructions and the wheel turned out to be the size of the wheel of a toy car. But it all had its own excitement. Everything seemed controlled by electronic instruments and navigational computers, and it took constant warning to keep the lad's itchy fingers off the buttons and levers.

Once out of the shelter of the harbour, however, his interest switched. The bows were ploughing into the heaving waves as we met the full force of the gale. He watched enthralled as the sea fountains shot over the fo'csle, spraying the bridge windows. That was the place to be, the upper deck where you could feel the gale and spray in your face and feel like a real sailor.

'Can we go out there, dad?' he asked.

So we did, with the ship rolling and plunging towards Cherbourg. To stay on our feet we had to lean at a 40-degree angle, but it was exhilarating as only a gale at sea can be.

Facing head on, gripping the rail over the bows, the boy could hardly get his breath. The wind was forcing it back down his throat. He turned towards me gasping but with sheer pleasure in his face. This was something for his holiday essay all right.

'Come on, time for lunch,' I said.

On our way back down the starboard side to the lounge, he shrieked with laughter and leaned steeply back against the wind. 'Look! I'm nearly lying flat!' he shouted. 'It could almost blow you right up in the air, couldn't it?'

No sooner had he said it than I had to grab him from taking off. He'd flung open his raincoat and gripped the edges with outstretched hands to form makeshift wings. He shot forwards with the sudden thrust, a moment that turned his expression into a mixture of amazed delight and fear.

'Don't do that!' I shouted, hauling him back. 'This gale will whip you into the air like a kite, you idiot!'

'Could it really?' he said, his eyes shining. Despite the momentary shock, the prospect of whizzing over the top of the ship's funnel like Batman had a powerful appeal.

'Of course it could! You've seen what hurricanes can do to houses and trees, haven't you, on films? You'd be a feather up there. Come on!'

We entered the tranquil air of the lounge. 'Christine, you should come out there! It's fantastic in the wind,' he said, 'I nearly turned into a kite!' But his enthusiasm fell on deaf ears. About the last thing Christine was interested in at that moment was boy kites. Her face had turned several shades whiter. She, too, lay slumped in the same posture of surrender as her mother.

'Anybody for lunch?' I said.

The Chief Fairy opened her eyes slowly. 'You've got to be joking,' she muttered and closed her eyes again.

'How much farther is it?' moaned Christine.

'There! Now who's moaning?' said Gavin triumphantly. 'It was different when I was carsick, wasn't it? Now you know what it's like!' He sat down. 'Can I have a Coke and a packet of crisps, dad?'

'Don't - you'll be ill again,' his mother groaned, her eyes still shut.

'Look who's talking!' he said. 'I'm all right and I want some crisps.' His mother was too weak to fight back and since I'll do anything for peace the best I could manage was 'You won't eat your lunch!'

'Of course I'll eat my lunch, I'm not like this lot! Just bring me *un Coke* and *les chips* - and, of course, whatever you want yourself!' he grinned. 'Mum's quickly changed her tune, hasn't she? She was all for coming on holiday so she could eat lots of food, and now she doesn't want it!'

But his triumphant cockiness was to be short-lived. A few minutes later, when I returned from the bar, and in the total absence of any conversation from his mother and sister, he'd had time to absorb some of the ghastly scene around him - white-faced passengers lolling in their seats or staggering suddenly for the lounge exits. And instead of the exhilarating gale in his face there now wafted to his nostrils a faintly nauseous tang that betokened human misery somewhere aboard the ship. It was carried across the heaving lounge by the ship's ventilation system.

'There you are,' I said, putting his Coke and crisps on the table. He muttered 'Thank you,' but didn't pick them up.

I sat down and raised my light ale. 'Cheers!' I said. He made no reply. Not only had a considerable amount of his jauntiness gone but there was also a definite pallor creeping into his face.

'You all right?' I said.

'Of course I'm all right,' he muttered.

At that moment the ship gave a violent lurch as a bigger wave than usual thumped its bows and sent a judder from stem to stern. An ashen-faced man groping his way past our table towards the exit suddenly sat down on a vacant chair. It was not so much voluntary, more a collapse as the deck fell away under his foot. He was clutching a white paper bag tightly in his hand, ready for emergency use.

Gavin looked across the table at him. The man bravely tried to smile. It would have been better had he not tried. It produced a ghastly effect on his green-tinged features.

Gavin tried to smile back, but the movement in his features - you could hardly call it a smile - flickered only briefly. Our new table companion began to gulp, wild-eyed, and staggered away clutching his bag to his mouth. Gavin groaned, 'Oh, God!J

'Are you sure you're all right, son?' I said.

'*I'm trying to be!*' he snapped. 'I was all right till I came in here. It's seeing all this lot rolling around that -'

Suddenly he stopped, gulped and displayed that wild-eyed misery that marks all sea-sick victims. 'Come on!' I said and grabbed his hand. We just made the loo in time.

4 French as she is Shrugged

It was a pale and queasy family that I drove off the ship and through the Customs checkpoint at Cherbourg dockyard three hours later. They all sat silent as we went through the formalities of passport and Customs control.

But happily, once outside the dock gates and into the old, grey-stone town, the feel of solid road beneath us had a swift, stabilising effect. The family began to perk up and take an interest in all things French around them.

We had just caught the beginning of the evening rush hour, and cars and bicycles seemed to be whizzing and honking at us from all directions.

I had two immediate problems. I wasn't at all sure of my way out of town; I was also trying to remember to drive on the right, a custom I always have difficulty with for the first few hours on Continental roads. In fact, we'd travelled only 50 yards from the dock gates when the Chief Fairy frowned and said: 'Shouldn't you be on the right?'

'Good Lord, yes!' I muttered and swung the car violently onto the other side of the road. 'If anybody spots me doing something stupid like that, let me know, will you?' That perked the family up some more, if only in the interests of self-preservation.

For a moment the thought flashed across my mind that I ought to let my wife take the wheel since she's used to driving on the right at home - though not, of course, with the approval of other road-users. However, I quickly dismissed the idea. I may not be the world's best driver, but I am certainly the world's worst passenger if she is driving. This is more a criticism of my cowardice than her motoring ability.

'Keep your eyes peeled for any road signs to Carteret. That's where we want to be,' I said as we pulled up at a junction controlled by a uniformed gendarme.

Hardly had I said it than Gavin said, 'Look, *boulangerie!*'

'Where?' I said, thinking for a moment that he'd spotted a road sign, but it was a shop sign he was pointing at.

'That means bakery, doesn't it?' he said.

'Yes.'

'What does that word next to it mean - patis. . .?'

'*Patisserie*,' said Christine. 'Pastry shop.'

The words acted like adrenalin on the Chief Fairy. She swung round to look and went weak at the sight of the shop window display of mouthwatering French pastries. 'Oh, don't they look gorgeous! Look at those eclairs!' she said with a little gulp. The whole display blotted out all recollection of her condition an hour earlier and forcefully reminded her that not only had she not eaten lunch but had been dieting for days for such a treat as this.

We were still looking into the window when I became aware of a fierce whistling somewhere in the street.

'Daddy, it's the gendarme!' Christine shouted. 'He's waving at us!' He was too. A small, moustachioed fellow, he was angrily gesticulating and pumping his arm for me to turn right. I wasn't at all sure that I wanted to turn right. I felt that I should be going straight on but I was now trapped in a right-hand lane and the gendarme, standing on his box in the middle of the junction, was determined that I should lead my file round the corner.

'Hey, he's great!' said Gavin, peering at the gendarme. 'He looks just like Charlie Chaplin!' It wasn't far off the mark. Apart from his physical similarity, he was full of jerky, excited movements. Still, maybe that's how French rush hours get you, and I certainly wasn't doing too well myself. For I seemed to be finding it impossible to make a left turn, a task not assisted by the unnerving chorus of 'Keep to the right!' whenever I wandered into the middle of the road, looking for a road sign.

Eventually, we were doing so many right turns we were in

grave danger of imitating the worzel-worzel bird and vanishing up our own exhaust pipe. The only alternative seemed to be to drive into the sea.

'I'd better get out and ask someone,' I said, stopping the car at last in a tiny square. I climbed out and spoke to a scruffy, dark-skinned fellow who was sweeping up cabbage leaves in front of a vegetable stall. Well - I say 'spoke', I flatter myself. I quickly realised that my French, never much good anyway, had been too long in cold storage. I'd got all the Gallic shrugs, the gestures, the expressive hands, the thrust of the eyebrows - all the facial language, in fact - but nothing was coming out between the lips.

I got as far as '*Pardon, m'sieu - er - um,*' then the grimaces took over, with the odd phrase suddenly blurted out. '*Voulez-vous* - um - *me dire* - um, er - *où se trouve* - the er - *la rue à Carteret?*' He had stopped sweeping up his cabbage leaves and was looking at me with interest. '*Eh? Hein? Alors?*' I added, more as makeweight for my atrocious accent.

He frowned and shook his head. 'Zorree, I not spik ze English,' he muttered. English my foot - that was my French!

'Doesn't he understand?' said Gavin when I returned.

'No.'

'I thought you could speak French,' he accused sternly.

'So did I,' I muttered, feeling a bit exposed. That's what comes of throwing in too much linguistic bravura across the breakfast table - '*Bonjour mes enfants! Ça va, mon vieux? Eh? Alors!*' It might fool your kids but not a real Frenchman sweeping up cabbage leaves.

'What were all those faces you were pulling then?' he demanded. 'I thought you were talking to him.'

This fruitless inquisition had gone on long enough. 'Look,' I said, 'there's obviously only one way to get out of this town and that's to start making some left-hand turns. We've got to break out of these ever-decreasing circles.'

'Haven't you got a map of the town?' asked the Chief Fairy.

'No, I haven't, otherwise I'd have used it, but don't worry, we'll get out of it now - it's not that big.'

With renewed determination I shoved the car into gear, shot out of the square and at last took a left turn in the midst of the traffic stream down what looked like a promising street.

'Good,' I said, 'now we're on the road. See? The sun's dead ahead - that's where we want to head for, south-west.'

My wife looked at me drily. She always does whenever I start using the sun or the stars as navigational bearings on the road. I don't know why, they're just as effective whether you're lost on the A30 or in the Atlantic, though I can never persuade her of this.

'There you are!' I added. I felt quite pleased with my victory - it shows, I thought, what simple determination will do - but hardly had I got the words out than a car came roaring towards us on our side of the road. I braked sharply, pulling into the kerb.

'What's the fool doing?' I exclaimed. 'He's driving on the left!'

'It's probably another Englishman,' said Gavin helpfully.

'Look at the idiot!' I said as he whizzed past, gesticulating and honking wildly. I pulled out again, but within seconds another maniac came at me and I had to swerve violently back to the kerb again. 'Are they all mad or something?' I said.

As if to confirm my suspicions there came a loud rap at my window and another Frenchman began to gesticulate and babble volubly at me.

'You'd better see what he wants, dear, there's obviously something wrong,' said the Chief Fairy. Once again I climbed out of the car. Since I was driving a Renault, the fellow clearly took me for another Frenchman and continued to babble at great speed, looking at me questioningly. I couldn't understand a word.

'*Parlez lentement, s'il vous plaît, m'sieu,*' I managed to say at last between more shrugs and grimaces. '*Je ne comprends pas.*'

'Ah!' he said, the light of recognition suddenly dawning at my amazing accent. He pointed down the street. 'Ees one-way street, m'sieu. You go ze wrong way!'

Well, at least that solved one mystery.

I backed out of the street, and mainly by a grinding process of elimination we found ourselves on the right road.

'There it is!' yelled Gavin, pointing to a sign. 'Carteret - 36km, whatever that means.'

'Thank heavens!' I said. 'It means 36 kilometres - about 26 miles.'

It was just after we'd passed our Charlie Chaplin gendarme for the third time. He was still whistling, pirouetting and gesticulating excitedly in his point-duty ballet and from the glare he gave us as he arm-pumped us round yet another corner it was just as well we didn't have to return for a fourth performance. He seemed to think it was some kind of plot to tire his arm out.

In an attempt to allay his suspicions I gave what I hoped was an apologetic Gallic shrug and with a weak smile raised my holiday hat to him, as we drove past his rostrum yet again. His whistle nearly fell out of his mouth.

'You shouldn't have done that!' scolded Gavin. 'He probably thinks you fancy him!'

At long last, we were clear of the town and heading southwest on a fast highway. As our speed increased so did our spirits. The family began pointing excitedly at features and characters of interest in the old, grey-stone villages that picturesquely dot the Normandy countryside. There was an air of timeless roots about the setting of centuries-old churches and cottages, and here and there a black-shawled peasant woman or an old farmer moving against the near-deserted landscape. In the evening sunshine the passing pastural scenes evinced something solidly French and nostalgic.

Our own buoyant spirits now caught the Gallic atmosphere and the kids broke into snatches of French songs - *Alouette*, *Frère Jacques* and *Au près de ma blonde* rolled out from the speeding car over the Normandy countryside. We all joined in.

Ahead of us, across the gently undulating Cotentin Peninsular, stretched mile after mile of long straight roads, which we were to find so much a feature of motoring through rural France. There's no doubt they help the touring motorist to gobble up distances at great speed if he feels inclined. Only one snag stands in his way - French signposting.

We had already found that unlike British roads, where plenty of advance warning is given for the motorist, directions to towns in France tend to get announced suddenly, without warning, at the very junction you need to turn off. But I had adjusted to that after twice being nearly deafened by shrieks in my ear from the back seat. 'That's the road, you've passed it!' as we shot past by-roads signposting our destination.

For me this adjustment was perhaps easier than for most since it was just like doing a shopping trip with my wife. I'm quite used to her suddenly shouting, 'That's the shop I want!' when I'm level with it in a busy road and doing 30 miles an hour. It happens all the time.

'Well, it won't be long now,' I said after our second turn-off and with only a few miles to go. 'At last, Gavin, you can say we're nearly there.'

It was now six o'clock and it seemed an age ago since he first asked me that question. It had been a long, eventful and exhausting day. Nor had it been helped by the moment of panic at Southampton Docks when we couldn't find - or rather, I couldn't find - our Green Card insurance cover. Only after turning the car almost inside out and searching every suitcase did I find it - in the inside pocket of a suit I'd packed at the bottom of the last case. For safe keeping, of course, what else?

But all these minor calamities, including the sea-sickness, were now behind us and once again I was glad I'd taken the precaution of booking ahead for our first overnight stop at Carteret. At least there should be no problem over accommodation.

'Will there be a beach at Carteret?' Gavin asked.

'I'm told there's a lovely beach,' I said. 'And a little harbour and fishing boats. Lots of French families go there.'

'If we like it can we stay an extra day?' said Christine excitedly. Like a woman she's a great one for planning her happiness insurance cover well ahead.

'I know what Christine's thinking of,' snorted Gavin. 'She's hoping to get off with a French boy in one of those families, so she can go snogging!'

'No I'm not!' she said.

'Oh yes you are!'

'I can't wait to get at that French food, I'm starving,' their mother sighed.

'So am I!' Gavin said, his interest in his sister's love life suddenly vanishing. 'I didn't have any lunch.'

'None of us did,' Christine said.

'Come to think of it,' said Gavin, leaning over my shoulder, 'you've had a pretty cheap day, haven't you? After all your moaning about the cost, you were the only one to eat lunch!'

'Well,' I said, 'since you've all starved to save my money you can have a treat tonight. You can splash out on whatever luxury dish you fancy.'

'Look out Carteret, here I come!' murmured the Chief Fairy.

'Me too!' said Christine.

'And me!' said Gavin.

'And me!' I said. There was a burst of laughter in the car. Suddenly all the tribulations of the day seemed to fall away. For the first time since leaving home that morning we felt a soaring sense of escape. The holiday had really begun.

5 'Ou Est le Loo?'

The family were enchanted with Carteret, a delightful little town of attractive houses, shops and summer places clustered round the tiny port - a haven, obviously, for yachtsmen. In a sheltered bay between rocky headlands lay a beach of fine sand backed by tempting sand dunes - a heaven, obviously, for children.

Small fishing boats and sailing dinghies bobbed about in the river estuary that divided the town from its twin resort of Barnetville, which was flatter, more open, but with its own magnificent stretch of beach. In the summer season a boat service ran daily to the off-shore island of Jersey, and by taking the morning ferry it was possible, my travel-writer friend had told me, to spend a good day on the island and return to Carteret or Barnetville in time for dinner.

As we pulled up on the grass verge outside our little sea-front hotel the children were all for exploring the place there and then. The gales had dropped, the clouds gone and the evening sun warm on our faces.

'Come on, Christine!' Gavin shouted. 'Let's climb the sand dunes!'

'Let's get checked into the hotel first,' I said, 'then you can explore.'

But inside the hotel a shock awaited us. We weren't booked in at all. *Non*, they knew nothing about us. *Non*, they had not received my letter. *Non*, it was very doubtful whether they had rooms to spare at such short notice. *Non*, cancellations were very rare.

'Oh, that's great,' said Gavin drily. 'Now we've got nowhere to sleep!'

However, *oui*, the receptionist would investigate. She would consult *Madame* and departed into distant regions behind the reception desk.

'I thought you'd booked all this up,' frowned the Chief Fairy. 'Didn't you get a reply back from them?'

'Don't forget we did all this in less than a week,' I reminded her. 'With our postal service there wouldn't have been time to get a reply back. My letter's obviously gone astray.'

'You did post it, I suppose?'

'Of course!' I thought for a moment. 'Well, Christine posted it for me, didn't you?'

'When?' frowned Christine.

'That day you took your library book back.'

Her fingers moved to her lips in quick apprehension.

'And you put it in the back of your library book!' said Gavin.

We all groaned.

'That's obviously where it still is - stuck in a book on the library shelves!' I said. 'Oh, well, it's no use bothering about it now. We'll have to start searching for somewhere else to stay the night.'

'Oh, Christine!' her mother scolded. 'You should pay more attention when you're asked to do something.'

'All right, I'm sorry,' she muttered.

'If you weren't wandering around in a dream . . .'

'All right, all right, I said I'm sorry, forget it!' she snapped.

A cloud had now descended on our spirits, which was a pity because only ten minutes earlier all had been joy and sunlight. If this hotel was full up it could well apply to the few others that were open out of season.

'We could always get the tent out, couldn't we?' said Gavin, brightening suddenly. 'We could pitch it on those sand dunes.'

'I'm not sleeping in any tent tonight, you can forget the idea,' I said.

'Neither am I,' Christine muttered. 'Not on our first night.'

'Well, it was your fault! You should have posted that letter!'

'Oh, shut up!' she said. 'Anyway, daddy said the tent was only in case of dire emergency.

We were very soon to find out whether this was to be such an emergency or not because through the door behind the reception desk walked *Madame*. She was a pleasant-looking woman in her thirties, who turned out to be the proprietor's wife, but who spoke not a word of English.

'*Ah, bonsoir, madame!*' I said. With much shrugging, gesticulating and using my facial French again, I tried to explain our predicament about the letter going astray, or rather not being posted. 'You see, *j'ai pensé* - that is, I thought - er - *nous avons réservé* - er - er - '

'*Une chambre!*' hissed Christine.

'*Oui, une chambre,*' I said. '*Merci,*' I added, turning unthinkingly to Christine, who promptly rolled her eyes heavenwards. 'I mean - here, look, don't you think you'd better do it? I mean your French must be better than mine - at least you are still learning it at school.'

'No, no, you do it!' she muttered, backing away and blushing. Kids, they never do what you want.

'Oh, very well,' I said and addressed myself again to *Madame*, who was now watching this little pantomime with mystified amusement. '*Nous avons réservé une chambre* no, hang on, I think I booked two rooms, at least I meant to - *deux chambres pour la nuit pour moi et ma famille*.'

'*Oui, je comprends, m'sieu,*' she smiled. '*Suivez-moi, s'il vous plaît!*' She moved towards the staircase. We watched with surprise.

'See! There you are, we've been worrying over nothing,' I said. 'She has rooms for us. Come on, she wants us to follow her.' I turned to Gavin. 'There you are, the old man's French isn't so bad after all.' He seemed unimpressed. I think he'd rather have had the tent.

Upstairs the proprietor's wife showed us two rooms, small but comfortable and one with a nice view over the harbour. How the rooms became suddenly available when the receptionist had indicated that it was highly doubtful any were vacant was just one of those mysteries that one is forever encountering in hotels. 'Fine - *bon, merci, Madame!*' I said.

'Ask her what time dinner is served,' said the Chief Fairy, who speaks no French at all.

'*À quelle heure,*' I began, then once again, searching for the words, resorted to mime. I made a knife and fork action. 'Er - *mangeons-nous?*'

Christine groaned. '*Mangeons-nous! À quelle heure est dîner servis!*'

'Look,' I said, aggrieved, 'I wish you'd do it instead of tearing my French apart!'

But the message had already come across to Madame. '*Ah! Dîner est servi à sept heures et demi, m'sieu,*' she replied.

'That's half-past seven,' Gavin said triumphantly. 'Come on, Christine, we can go and explore for half an hour!'

'Don't go far . . . ' their mother began, but they'd already shot out of the door - Christine, I think, with embarrassment. *Madame* turned to follow them.

'Ask her where the loo is,' muttered the Chief Fairy. 'We've got a shower and wash basin but no loo.'

Her spirits had taken a temporary down-turn at the discovery of this omission in our quarters because, as brief a time as we had been in France, we had already had some trouble over French plumbing. Lavatories seemed few and far between and where they could be found for general public use seemed woefully lacking in style and hygiene.

'*Ou est la* - um - *salle de bain?* Bathroom?' I asked *Madame*.

She frowned, puzzled, then drew back the shower curtain. '*Voila, m'sieu!*'

'No - *non* - I mean le loo, *la toilette,*' I discreetly pulled an imaginary chain. Her eyes followed my arm movement, then brightened suddenly.

'*Ah, oui, je comprends, m'sieu, par ici, suivez-moi!*' She led us down to a loo at the end of the corridor. It looked clean and adequate, if rather a long way from our base. The Chief Fairy breathed again and gave *Madame* a little smile. 'Mercy,' she murmured, which was not intended to indicate that such a hygienic loo was a blessing, though it was; it was intended to express her gratitude in the one word of French she had now learned, even if the pronunciation was a bit sketchy. *Madame* smiled back and left.

Three-quarters of an hour later, after a quick shower and an aperitif in the bar, we sat down in the restaurant. 'Oh, did you catch that gorgeous smell as we came past the kitchen?' said the Chief Fairy. 'I wonder what's on the menu?'

As if in answer, a waitress appeared almost at once and passed out four menus. 'Mercy,' murmured the Chief Fairy again.

But her eyes glazed over as she stared at the night's list of runners. 'It looks marvellous, but I can't understand a word of it!'

'Neither can I,' said Gavin. 'It's all in funny writing. I can't even read it!'

He had a point. Not for the first time I found myself thinking that handwritten French menus all seem to be scrawled by the same cramped hand, with loops and twirls and jammed-up letters. After a moment I managed to decipher some of it.

'Well, I can see lamb there for a start - *l'agneau.* And trout - *truite.* And veal - *veau.* And fillet of beef - *boeuf.*'

'And chicken,' said Christine. '*Poulet.*'

'I'll have chicken and chips,' said Gavin, throwing aside his menu.

'Oh, but you always have chicken and chips at home,' protested his mother, who constantly tries to guide his palate off things he loves into fancy culinary adventures which he can't stand. 'Wouldn't you like to try something really French?'

'Chicken and chips,' he said emphatically, folding his arms to indicate the discussion was now at an end. 'You have something French if you want it.'

His mother looked doubtfully back at the menu.

'I'll have chicken, too,' said Christine, '*avec les pommes frites et petits pois.*'

'*Escalope de veau pour moi,*' I said.

'I wish I could understand it all,' groaned the Chief Fairy.

'I mean I wish I knew how it was all done, what the sauces are and how it's been cooked.'

I could tell by the tormented frown on her face that she was afraid of choosing the wrong thing when she had such a marvellous appetite to do justice to the right dish. Happily, at that moment, the proprietor approached our table with the wine list, and as we had already learned over our aperitif in the bar, he spoke quite good English. A handsome, rather charming fellow.

'Ah, m'sieu,' I said, 'I wonder if you could explain some of these dishes on the menu for my wife.'

'Certainly,' he said with a smile, and bending down beside her proceeded through every item, detailing how it was cooked, in what wine and what sauce and what trimmings went with it.

As he lovingly and with expressive gestures read out and described each dish, in his even more expressive French accent, the Chief Fairy's eyes became not only glazed but hypnotised. She went positively weak at the knees. It was as near a pornographic reading of a menu as you could get.

At the end of it she looked into his eyes and gulped. 'Oh, it sounds absolutely fantastic!'

'Good, *bon, madame,*' he said. 'So what would you like?'

'I'll start with the *vanneaux,*' she whispered, and gulped again.

'*Oui, bon, très délicieuse,*' he said, making a note of the order.

'I'll start with that, too,' I said, a bit hoarsely. He'd sold it to me too, and no mistake. It sounded like the food of the Gods the way he put it across - a plate of tiny, freshly-caught, local clams, cooked in butter, parsley, garlic and onion and served hot, open in the shell.

'And for the children?'

He took the rest of our order, recommended a good bottle from his wine list and departed to the kitchen to hustle the feast. And what a feast! No experience could have proved a better start to our French holiday. It was a truly magnificent meal, each flavour delicately and lovingly nursed in every dish, and each course surpassing its predecessor. At the end of it you just had to recognise the yawning gap between English and French cooking, even at a small family hotel like this. Even the children, to whom food is usually just food, went into raptures over the manner in which their chicken had been prepared. As for the *vanneaux*, which we had never tasted before, it did such exquisite things to the palate you felt positively sinful. The Chief Fairy swore she'd never had a meal like it.

At the end of it, with about 4,000 extra calories struggling against her girdle, she walked dreamily out of the restaurant past the politely bowing proprietor. 'Mercy,' she said, 'Mercy. It was fantastic.' Nothing warms the personality more than a splendid meal.

'I'm so pleased *Madame* enjoyed it,' he smiled. 'Perhaps a coffee and cognac in the bar?'

She looked at him as though he were all the Romeos of the ages. What charm! What attentiveness! What understanding!

In the bar she said to me: 'What was that he murmured as he put down that *vanneaux* in front of me?'

'Mm? Oh, *bon appetit*. Good appetite - enjoy your meal.'

She sighed. 'Oh, do let's stay another night!'

Truly, as Shaw said, there is no love sincerer than the love of food. She never drools over me like that.

6 Bong Goes her Diet

The next day dawned hot and bright, with a gentle April breeze blowing across the bay. It was a perfect day for a picnic.

The Chief Fairy and I were hardly awake when the kids burst into our room. They were fully dressed and had already been out on the sand dunes. 'We *are* staying, aren't we?' said Gavin enthusiastically. 'You said we could stay another day if we wanted to.'

'Well, if there's a majority vote that we stay another day,' I said, heaving myself up in bed, 'then we stay another day. Hands up those who want to stay.'

The kids' hands shot up. I glanced at their mother, half-dozing beside me. Her eyes were closed, but the same dreamy smile of the night before was playing at her lips. There was little doubt what she had been dreaming about.

'How about you?' I said. Without a word, or flicker in her smile, her hand rose in assent from the bedclothes. 'Okay,' I said, 'we stay another night.'

'What about you, daddy, do you want to stay?' Christine asked.

'Sure, it's fine by me,' I said. After the gales of the day before it was much too nice a day to waste behind the wheel of a car. We could press on with our journey tomorrow.

'Can we go down to the beach then and take our swimming things?' said Gavin.

'We could picnic down there if you like,' I said.

'Oh, yes!' the kids chorused.

At the word 'picnic' the Chief Fairy's eyes shot open.

'We could buy some stuff at those shops we passed near the harbour,' she said. 'Some French bread and cheese and wine and . . .'

'And Coke and crisps! *Les chips!*' interrupted Gavin excitedly, leaping up and down on the bed.

'And some French pâté and pastries,' said the Chief Fairy, sitting up and now wide awake.

'Aye-aye, she's off!' I said. 'Come on, let's get dressed and go down to breakfast first!'

As we entered the terraced, sunlit restaurant the aroma of percolating coffee, French rolls and warm croissants put her back on Cloud Seven again. 'Oh, can you smell that? It's just too gorgeous!' she sighed. 'If you've got to go off a diet this is the only way to go!'

It tasted every bit as good as it smelled, too - particularly the coffee. 'No one in the world makes coffee like the French,' declared the family's refugee from a calorie counter. She blissfully poured herself a second cup, while the kids tucked into the buttered rolls and *confiture*.

'Right,' I said at the end of the meal, 'now for a brisk walk down the sea-front to the High Street shops and we'll try out our French on the *boulangerie*, *patisserie* and *charcuterie*. Oui? *Bon!*'

'What's a *charcuterie?*' said Gavin.

'It's where they sell the cooked meats and pates and cheeses which will shortly have your mother swooning again,' I said. 'Come on!'

'I want to buy some cards to send home,' said Christine. 'Can I have my pocket money now, in francs?'

I began to fish in my pocket.

'Me, too!' said Gavin, who never misses a trick. 'You owe me for last week, too. You didn't pay me!' I'm always owing him for last week. I'm always never paying him, he says. I keep vowing to introduce a system of receipts but somehow I never get round to it. He'd be a sensation at the Exchequer.

'Okay,' I said, doling out the equivalent francs.

'What rate of exchange are you giving me?' he demanded suspiciously. 'There's only - let me see - 7 francs here!'

'That's the best rate you'll ever get for sterling over here!' I retorted. 'The official rate is only 12 francs to the pound. I'm giving you 7 francs for your 50p pocket money, which is 14 francs to the pound. I must be mad.'

'Oh, that's all right,' he said, grudgingly. I repeat he'd be a wow as Chancellor of the Exchequer. 'Come on, then, let's get *les chips!*' he shouted, running out to the sea-front.

We followed and turned towards the little street of shops at the end of the harbour wall, a quarter of a mile away. It was a beautiful day - seagulls wheeling in the sun and sails bobbing on the sparkling waters of the estuary. As we stepped out along the sea-front the Chief Fairy looked down at her figure. 'See?' she said, pleased and thumbing the belt of her pretty summer frock, 'Not an inch of damage yet!'

'Let's see you do that again in a fortnight,' I said.

'Oh, shut up!' she said, giving a little skip and taking my arm. 'I've gone through tortures for this treat. Don't ruin it!'

'Oh, blimey, you're talking about diets again, are you?' groaned Gavin and ran on ahead to peer over the harbour wall at a fishing boat loading up crab creels. Christine turned her face to the warm sun, closing her eyes briefly. 'Doesn't it feel marvellous?' she said. 'I'm going to put on my bikini when we get down to the beach. I want to go back with a fantastic tan.'

The high street was already busy with a sprinkling of early morning shoppers and bakery and grocery delivery vans. We stopped to look first at a little souvenir shop with picture postcards, buckets, spades and other seaside things hanging outside.

As we were looking in the window Christine selected four cards from the rack and walked boldly into the shop. 'Are you going to ask for them yourself in French?' whispered Gavin, following her in with slightly amazed admiration. I moved to the door to see what happened.

'Of course I am,' she retorted confidently. Turning to the woman assistant behind the counter, she said, '*Combien pour quatre cartes postales, s'il vous plaît?*'

'*Deux francs, mam'selle.*'

'*Et avez-vous des timbres aussi, madame?*'

'*Oui, mam'selle!*' replied the woman with a smile, and proceeded to tear off four stamps for her. It was too much for Gavin. He dashed out of the shop door, nearly knocking me over.

'Here!' he said. 'Christine's talking French! She has just bought some cards and stamps!'

'Fantastic,' I said, at his expression of incredulity. 'But isn't that what she's learning at school, like you?'

It was obvious that he had not seriously related the French spoken in school - and the bravura rubbish by me over the breakfast table - with anything actually spoken by people in French shops. And certainly my own stumbling, grimacing and shoulder-shrugging display since our arrival had done nothing to change that opinion.

As Christine came out of the souvenir shop he offered her his francs. 'Will you ask for some crisps for me, Christine?' he said.

'Ask for them yourself,' she said.

He hesitated. 'What do I say? - *Avez-vous les chips?*'

'Yes.'

'Is that all?'

'Yes.'

'All right,' he said, then stopped at the door. 'Will you come in with me in case I get stuck?'

'How can you get stuck over "*avez-vous les chips?*"' retorted Christine.

'But she might say something I don't understand!' he said, looking worried. 'Come on, Christine - please!'

He didn't, I noticed, ask me to accompany him, which showed pretty conclusively where his confidence lay in the family linguistics. He'd seen a practical demonstration which, unlike mine, actually worked.

'Oh, all right,' said Christine, 'but you can do it perfectly well yourself.'

I hovered at the door again - but less now out of idle curiosity, more out of educational opportunity. Who knows? I might learn some French from my kids.

Inside the shop Gavin held out his small fistful of francs and timidly addressed the lady at the counter. '*Avez-vous les chips?*'

'Ah,' she said, giving him a little regretful smile, '*pas ici, mon petit, mais au premier magasin à gauche.*'

Gavin was still holding out his fistful of francs but his arm began to waver a bit when he saw that she was making no move to hand him his crisps. He turned angrily to Christine. 'There! I told you she'd say something I didn't understand! What's she on about?'

Christine, who had been frowning, deep in thoughtful translation, now worked out the answer. 'She says they don't sell crisps here but you can buy them at the first shop on the left.'

'Oh, come on then!' he said irritably and strode out of the shop. This time, in a slight mood of aggression, he marched into the next shop without asking for any support and came out a minute later beaming and holding his prize of a packet of crisps.

'*Regardez!*' he said triumphantly, then offered the packet round. 'Have *un chip!*'

There was a village friendliness about the High Street, bathed now in the warm morning sun. It was a friendliness accentuated by the French custom of hand-shaking. Shopkeepers, delivery men and pedestrians seemed to be doing it all over the place, much to Gavin's wonderment.

'Why is everybody shaking hands?' he said. 'They were doing it in our restaurant this morning, too.'

'The French always do it. It's a national custom,' Christine said, a bit loftily I thought, since her own acquaintance with it was hardly extensive - gained, in fact, from one day trip to Boulogne and a short school journey. However, in the oneupmanship game between brother and sister even the tiniest edge of superiority must be pressed home.

'Oh, you know everything, don't you?' said Gavin, stuffing himself with more crisps.

'Actually, I think it's rather a nice custom,' said the Chief Fairy. 'Everybody shaking hands when they meet in the morning, it sort of sets the day off in a nice cosy fashion.'

'Yes, well, if it stopped with the morning it would be all right,' I said, 'but it goes on day and night. If they go to the loo they come back shaking hands. Your arm can get tired out.'

In fact, I once knew a fellow - a big, cheerful, noisy chap, he was - who spent a year in France and returned to England with an incurable dose of it. He couldn't stop shaking hands with people. Each day he'd enter his office building booming '*Bonjour*' at everybody and grabbing their hands. He couldn't sit down at his desk without going round the whole floor and shaking hands with the whole staff, from office boys to executives, even total strangers. If they happened to be walking down the corridor he'd reach for their hand and boom, '*Ah, bonjour!*' There was nothing else wrong with him, of course, he was quite efficient, but that year in France had given him a galloping attack of the shakes. You started taking your hand out of your pocket the moment you saw him coming towards you.

The office eventually retired him - giving him a golden handshake, of course.

'Oh, look! Here we are!' said the Chief Fairy, stopping suddenly in front of a patisserie window. 'Just look at those!' She gazed enraptured at the display of fresh croissants, pastries, gateaux and éclairs. 'Oh, come on, let's get some for the picnic.' In we went.

She moved round the shelves, selecting with wide-eyed delight like a slave let loose in Aladdin's cave of treasures. I acted as interpreter, which mainly amounted to following her pointing finger and asking the charming patisserie assistant, '*Combien?*'

Since we were talking in francs and centimes it didn't mean very much to the calorie slave running amok among the treasures. Only when we got outside again did she start frowning over her sums. 'Sixteen francs? How much is that?'

'About thirty-three bob,' I said.

'Thirty-three bob! For pastries! Good Heavens!'

'And French bread and croissants,' I said. 'But never mind, let's not stint on our first picnic.'

Her shock at French food prices lasted about one minute - just long enough for us to reach the charcuterie shop window, where her eyes fell on the pates, cold meats and cheeses. We packed our picnic bag with a supply of these, too, and from a small supermarket round the corner bought a bottle of *Côte du Rhône* to wash it down. At three francs - about 25p - it was the best bargain of the lot, a fact we were happy to marvel at several times in the course of the day - and particularly while drinking it on the sand dunes with our picnic.

'Isn't that marvellous?' I said. 'Only five bob for a bottle of beautiful red wine like that!' Our pleasure, of course, had some of the philosophy of the ostrich about it because, with our heads in the bottle, as it were, it conveniently helped us to forget the cost of the other picnic items, which worked out about £1 a head.

This ostrich was eventually to come home to roost calamitously - but that, if I may stir the metaphors once more, was not even a small cloud on the horizon yet.

All that day we sunbathed, swam and picnicked on the sand dunes. It was an idyllic day and did wonders for everybody's spirits after the gales and exhausting Channel crossing of the day before. While we relaxed under the warm April sun I took the opportunity to brush up on my rusty French. On our little shopping trip I had bought an English-French phrase book. I hadn't realised just how much I had forgotten - not that my French was ever any great shakes. In fact, it once lost us a marvellous *au pair* girl called Monique, and I didn't want any similar problems to arise.

Sweet 17 and a pretty thing, too, Monique came to stay with

us in London to help with the children and learn English. Her knowledge of the language at this time was almost nil, and the morning after she arrived I met her in the kitchen, where the Chief Fairy was trying to communicate with her. My wife's way of communicating in a language she doesn't understand is to open her eyes wide, and talk slowly and loudly in English, as though to a backward child.

'*Bonjour,*' I said.

'*Bonjour, m'sieu!*' said Monique, turning to me with a deeply grateful smile. At last, a word she understood!

'*Et comment ca va aujourd'hui?*' I said, with more of my breakfast-time bravura. She smiled brightly again and said, thank you, she went fine today.

Encouraged by this success, I ventured to find something more ambitious to say, while the Chief Fairy looked on a bit lost. Monique gazed at me expectantly. Had she, I asked, had a good night's sleep. Her expression changed to one of slight surprise and she blushed, lowering her eyes, saying nothing.

Well, I repeated, yes or no?

She glanced, a little anxiously I thought, towards my wife, then gave a little shrug. '*Oui, m'sieu,*' she murmured.

'*Bon,*' I said, and she blushed again, giving another slightly apprehensive look towards my wife, who began to look puzzled. I, too, was a little puzzled by her manner and it was not until that evening I discovered why. I had used the wrong verb - '*coucher*' instead of '*dormir*' - and what I had asked our cute little *au pair* girl was not had she had a good night's sleep, but was she good in bed!

It was over dinner with neighbours that this gaffe of mine was laid bare and a helpful expert in the language smilingly put me right, saying: 'Of course, what's interesting about that exchange is that she told you, yes, she was good in bed!' The Chief Fairy was not amused. I won't say she took active steps to pack her off back to France but for several days afterwards she kept saying how difficult and inconvenient it was to communicate with her helper. It was nothing against Monique, you understand, but maybe we might do better with an *au pair* who at least had some knowledge of English.

When I ribbed her about it she said, coolly: 'I am no more put out by it than you would be if, say, it had been a French *au pair* man whom I had asked was he good in bed and he had said yes he was, and I had said, "Bon!" We could all live happily with that under the same roof, couldn't we?'

I decided it was politic not to pursue the matter and thereafter left Monique's sleeping arrangements totally out of all breakfast-time conversations. After a month she left of her own accord, anyway, which was just as well. Whether it had been my imagination or not, I don't know, but it seemed as the days went by I was getting a lot of 'come hither' looks and secret smiling in the region of the bedrooms. She finally left - to return to 'ze boy frand', apparently pining for her back in Rheims - and no doubt much mystified by the English husband full of such bold promise and so backward in coming forward.

Back in the hotel that night we dined again on another selection of superb dishes, but starting off once again with those exquisite *vanneaux*. This time, when the waitress came up with the menu, we didn't need the services of an interpreter, and we made our choices from the memory of his descriptions the night before. Only Gavin ran into a small problem. He said he wanted chicken again but this time he wanted the wing not the leg. The waitress looked puzzled as I tried to interpret this into French. '*Poulet, oui*,' I said, 'but he wants, what's the French for wing?' She stood frowning, mystified. '*Pas la jambe*, not the leg,' I went on, then pulled out my phrase book to search for 'wing'. I couldn't find it.

Suddenly Gavin had an inspiration, tapped the waitress to draw her attention to himself then began to flap his arm up and down, making a clucking sound. He pointed urgently to his flapping arm, and I thought for a moment he was complaining about his sunburn.

'*Ah, oui!' L'aile du poulet. Je comprends!*'

'That's it, wing!' said Gavin. And up came the wing.

'Bong!' he said happily.

'*Bon appetit!*' replied the waitress.

'Mercy,' said the Chief Fairy, smiling at her.

Our French was coming along famously.

7 In Search of More Loos

It was just as well we stayed the extra day at Carteret and enjoyed the sun and the beach because the following morning dawned grey and windy, with rain clouds skudding in west from the Atlantic. It was a day for travelling.

We said our goodbyes to Monsieur le Patron and his wife, who had been so kind to us at their family hotel, and headed south for Dinard, where we hoped to spend the night. Our plan was to drive leisurely along the lesser used coastal road so that we could take in the seaside and rural scenery, rather than follow the main road. We could pick it up again at Avranches, about 100 kilometres south, then turn west into Brittany for another 80 kilometres or so to St. Malo and Dinard.

There I hoped to find the small quayside hotel where I had stayed with my own family as a child before the war - if it still existed.

On our way out of Carteret we stopped once again to buy food and another bottle of wine. We could picnic on the journey, but whether we would be able to eat in the open, as we had done the day before, was another matter. The weather didn't look at all promising. Still, we could always eat in the warmth of the car, and in any event the weather was having no depressing effect on the family. There was, once again, only a mood of excited anticipation.

Soon we were bowling along the almost deserted country roads, dipping down into little valleys then rising again to glimpse the sea and here and there a shuttered summer house. French music had started up in the back seat, but this time Christine was strumming her guitar and Gavin blowing away at his melodica as they fought to master '*Alouette*' and '*Au près de ma blonde*.' Many a cud-chewing cow looked over the hedges in bovine mystery as this moving cacophony passed by.

For an hour and a half or so we drove south in this fashion, enjoying the drive and the changing scene despite the rain which had now begun to lash down from the solid grey clouds racing in over the sea. Then came the first hint of our day's problems.

'I want to go to the loo,' said Gavin.

We were travelling at the time along a rather bleak stretch of empty road with flat open farmland on each side. A low hedge - little more than tall stubble really - ran on each side of the road, but there wasn't a tree in sight. For a moment or so we drove on in silence. 'I want to go to the loo!' repeated Gavin firmly.

'Yes, I heard you the first time,' I said. 'I was looking for a convenient spot but I can't see one. Never mind . . . ' I braked the car and pulled into the side of the road. 'You can hop out here, there's no one about.'

'I'm not going out there to do it,' he said, 'someone might come along!'

'You're in France now,' I said, 'they don't bother about these things.'

'Well, I do!' he protested hotly. 'I think it's disgusting! Can't you find a pub or something?'

He had already observed several times, with some astonishment, motorists and passengers calmly peeing by the roadside, next to their stationary vehicles, and making no attempt to conceal the fact. The first time came as a bit of a shock to him. As we passed a motorist leisurely watering his horse on a fairly busy section of the main road just outside Cherbourg, Gavin exclaimed. 'Hey, look at him! Piddling in the middle of the road!' He swung round to look out of the back window as our car drove on. 'He wasn't even standing by a hedge or anything!'

'Yes,' agreed the Chief Fairy, 'they don't seem to care.'

I told her that such public immodesty was rated somewhat lower on the French worry-scale of priorities than a full bladder, and we would probably encounter quite a lot of that sort of thing. We did.

On a quiet stretch of road just before we entered Carteret we passed a rather fat woman unselfconsciously squatting beside her parked car. 'Cor!' said Gavin, amazed again. 'Look at her flashing her bare bum!'

The Chief Fairy at once scolded him for his immoderate language, but this one was too much for him and despite the wigging he burst out laughing, rolling about in the back seat.

'There's an item for your holiday essay,' I said.

'Not likely!' he retorted. 'I'd get told off if I put that in!'

'You will if you use expressions like that,' his mother said.

But none of this had yet helped him to readjust his own British-orientated standards to the French custom. 'You might as well go on,' he said now, 'because I'm not getting out here. Look, there's another car just passing us! Hurry up, will you, and find somewhere else!'

A note of urgency had crept into his voice. His problem wasn't being helped by the swish of the rain outside and the sight of the water running down the windows. 'All right,' I said, pushing the car into gear again, 'maybe we'll find a village ahead.'

We were now on the coastal stretch between the seaside town of Granville and Avranches. The Chief Fairy, who was acting as map-reader, consulted the map on her knee and said: 'According to this there should be a place about four miles ahead.'

'Four miles!' Gavin groaned. 'I can't wait that long!'

I glanced over the navigator's shoulder. 'That's not miles, that's kilometres,' I said. 'It's just over two miles.'

'Oh, sorry,' said the Chief Fairy.

Sure enough in a few minutes we came upon a small hamlet with a cafe-bar on the left. 'This'll do,' I said, pulling up outside.

We all entered the rather old, low-beamed building, where attempts had been made to modernise it inside. There was a bar, two or three tables and a pin-ball machine.

'Where is it?' Gavin hissed.

'Probably in the back,' I said. 'Just a sec, I'd better order something first. We can't all pile off the road and into his loo without buying something.'

A thin, swarthy, middle-aged Frenchman was standing behind the bar watching us with curious eyes and polishing a glass. Two customers were seated on stools in front of him, nursing their drinks, but their conversation had died as we walked in.

I asked for two cokes and two coffees and cognacs, then added, '*Où se trouve la toilette?*'

He nodded to a side door, which led out to the back. 'Away you go,' I said to Gavin. A minute or two later, as we sipped our coffee and cognac, he came back with his face as black as thunder. 'What a crummy loo!' he said.

'Ssh!' said the Chief Fairy, casting an apprehensive glance over her shoulder towards the swarthy bartender. 'They might speak English.'

'Well, you should see it!' he muttered. 'A hole in the ground with a brick wall round it and a chain over your head and water sloshing round everywhere!'

I gave an involuntary laugh, he looked so angry.

'It's not funny, you know!' he said.

'Is the ladies out there, too?' asked Christine.

'Ladies? What are you talking about? That's the same one for everybody! It's the only one!'

'Are you sure?' his mother asked nervously.

'Go and see for yourself if you don't believe me.'

'I don't think I'll bother,' muttered his mother, but Christine rose to inspect the offending loo. 'I'm not using that!' she declared emphatically when she came back. 'Anybody could wander in.'

'I'll keep guard if you like,' said Gavin chivalrously.

'You needn't bother, thanks. I think it's revolting too.'

'Let's move on, I think,' said the Chief Fairy. 'We'll find somewhere else.'

We stopped at two more rural cafe-bars before we found a

loo to their liking at a hotel in Avranches. Each time we stopped I felt it necessary to order a drink, and the thought occurred to me that I could get smashed off my head every day searching for a usable loo. Not only that, the more we drank in search of a loo the more we needed to look for another one! The whole system was self-perpetuating, and - in the apparent total absence of any public lavatories with passable standards of hygiene - one could see immediately why the French favoured the popular custom of peeing in the road.

Nor was I yet taking into account the financial hazard of this system of gaining relief for my family. With the morning's drinks of Cokes, coffees, brandies and a couple of red wines, calling at the loo had cost me nearly a couple of quid!

We eventually reached Dinard late in the afternoon after making two minor detours and stopping for our picnic within sight of a large, convenient hedge. The wind and rain had subsided now but it was still overcast, so we ate our French bread, pâté, cheese and wine in the car. Our first detour was to visit Mont-St-Michel, the ancient abbey that rises, as though from the page of a fairybook, in the middle of a sandy bay. The narrow cobbled streets twisting up to the abbey are a paradise for the souvenir hunter. A few miles farther on we turned off to visit the ancient, ramparted port of St. Malo, whose similarly narrow, cobbled streets I had once strolled through as a boy, with my mother and father. It is a town of great charm, character and history and I was delighted to see that it had apparently come through the war unscathed.

For an hour or so we wandered round its bustling, winding streets and little squares, collecting more postcards on the way, then returned to the car. I was anxious now to see if I could find the hotel where I had stayed in that summer holiday before the war.

All that I remembered across the years was that it was near a tall viaduct, close to the St. Malo ferry point and that somewhere near it was a swimming pool that had been formed on the rocks, so that when the tide came in it filled the pool. These were vague impressions distorted by time, rather than clear-cut images, and I wasn't really sure I would find the hotel at all. But I knew if I did, the moment I saw it I would remember it.

We had had a very happy holiday there, where in retrospect all the days seemed bathed in sunlight. I remembered the warmth of the sea for swimming and the wide sandy beach, and possibly more clearly than anything else the high diving board at the swimming pool. I had taken a picture of my older brother doing a swallow dive from the top board and it was still somewhere among the old snapshots and souvenirs in a cupboard at home.

They say you should never go back, but I'm glad I did. We drove around the streets of Dinard for half an hour searching in vain for my little hotel. We were almost on the point of giving up when suddenly a certain conjunction of streets stirred a memory in me. I climbed out of the car and on an impulse walked a short way down a side street. I was on top of the viaduct, looking down, and there it was below!

I hurried back to the car. 'I've seen it!' I said, and the family sensed my elation.

'Where?' Gavin asked.

'Just where I thought it would be!' I said. 'But we'll have to go back down the road we've come up to get below the bridge.' As we did so other familiar landmarks came into view - and there was the open air swimming pool with the diving board! It was just as I remembered it from 35 years ago, with the same back drop of cliffs. My sense of excitement and pleasure grew even more as I turned the car under the bridge and pulled up in front of the hotel. It was all the same. Nothing in this quiet little corner had changed. Above the hotel terrace ran the balcony off the bedrooms. Everything came back to me.

'That's the room my brothers and I shared!' I said, pointing to the end one on the balcony. 'I remember it! I wonder if it's vacant?'

'We'd better see if they can put us up, hadn't we?' said the Chief Fairy, but I was in no doubt now that they could. And, yes, the two end rooms were vacant. As we signed in I chatted to the proprietor and his wife and told them of my visit there before the war. They listened with interest to my stumbling French, and said but of course it was long before their time, though, strangely, the hotel had changed hands only three times in all those years, including the war years.

Some alterations had been made downstairs, mainly improving the restaurant and bar, but the rooms upstairs and the balcony overlooking the little ferry point were just as I remembered them.

Would we like dinner the proprietor's wife asked after she had shown us to our rooms? 'Yes,' I said, 'but first we'd like to clean up, then perhaps an aperitif in the bar?'

'*Oui, m'sieu,*' she smiled.

For a moment I stood happily contemplating my victory in not only finding the hotel but actually standing now where I had stood so long ago as a small boy in this place so distant from my childhood home, and unvisited since. Memories flooded back: the morning sun streaming through the balcony windows, my own laughter and excitement with my brothers, playing, slipping into our trunks to go swimming, bringing in shells from the beach, rushing down each morning so as not to miss any of the day, and hearing my father order our breakfast in his own excellent French.

My reverie was interrupted by an urgent tug at my sleeve. It was Gavin. 'Ask her where the loo is,' he muttered, 'I haven't seen it yet.'

Good thinking! '*Où se trouve la toilette, madame?*' I asked.

'*Ah, oui, m'sieu,*' she said, '*par ici,*' and led the way out of the bedroom down the corridor. What took her somewhat by surprise was the four-member inspection committee which followed her and which peered over her shoulder as she opened the loo door. '*Voila!*' she said. We sighed. It was clean and comfortable.

'Thank God for that,' muttered Christine.

'*Bon,*' I said to *Madame*.

'Bong!' agreed Gavin approvingly.

'Mercy,' smiled the Chief Fairy and we all trooped back to our rooms, leaving *Madame* slightly perplexed at such a full-scale inspection of her smallest room.

The fact was that plumbing facilities were now looming very large indeed in our list of priorities, and the words '*Où se trouve la toilette?*' were to become almost our theme song for the whole journey. Nor, we discovered, was our concern exclusive to us. It seemed that wherever two or more English people were gathered together the subject of French loos came up. Each one had his or her own tale of horror. Indeed, that very morning in the bar of the hotel in Avranches, where facilities had at last come up to the family's requirements, we met an English couple who had been having similar problems.

Once, in despair at not being able to find a hygienic public convenience in the villages they passed through, they had stopped beside a field of tallish grass, with a narrow path running through it. The wife went into the field and with much relief got down to her task. But what she failed to realise was that the same path could also be used by pedestrians and cyclists.

While she was still squatting a railway worker cycled past and courteously raised his cap. '*Bonjour, madame!*' he greeted her. The astonished wife, still crouching, looked up and went the colour of beetroot.

Her husband, who had been telling the story at the bar, laughed. 'She's still suffering from the shock, aren't you, love?' We laughed, too, but his wife didn't. It was apparent she would rather he had kept the tale to himself. He coughed a little guiltily and, presumably by way of atonement, launched into an attack on the whole French plumbing system.

'I mean, what I don't understand,' he said, 'is what the French have got against decent public loos. They've got a beautiful country, magnificent food, unbeatable wine, but where can your average tourist in the provinces find a simple, sanitary, hygienic public convenience? Nowhere! No wonder the French dash around everywhere with knitted brows and anxious faces. They can't find one either.'

We nodded agreement. Encouraged, he took another gulp at his scotch - his own ticket to a decent hotel loo - and went on, 'Oh, sure, they've got those occasional, mind-bending, medieval holes in the ground, which leave any civilised visitor staring about him in horror, and those other things in wrought-iron, like open-plan side-shows in the streets for *Les Hommes*. But nowhere the facilities that wouldn't make a bog peasant's toes curl.'

Gavin, who was sipping his fourth Coke of the day - his own pass to the hotel's loo - agreed vigorously. 'You get your feet wet, too,' he said.

Our chatty bar companion nodded. 'Even in the hotels, where at least the standard improves, one W.C. every 16 rooms seems to be regarded as sufficient. And as if that isn't bad enough you're forever having to search for secret buttons, plungers, levers and trip hammers. There's rarely anything as simple as a chain.'

What the French needed more than anything else, we decided, was a Minister of Plumbing to attend to these matters - *tout de suite*. If there was a touch of smugness in our criticism, at least we knew we could flush with pride in dear old England . . .

8 Crabs and Collywobbles

Dinard turned out to be just as exciting for my children as it had been for me as a boy, but for different reasons, as we shall see. However, the day was not to end without its setbacks.

After we had unpacked our overnight things and cleaned up we trooped down to dinner. Once again the menu was written in that same cramped scrawl that seems to write all French menus. But at least we were growing used to it and were now becoming familiar with the dishes. This time there were no *vanneaux* starters, but there was crab.

'That's for me,' I said. 'It'll be local crab, fresh out of the bay. Shellfish is a speciality in this area. I'll bet they do it marvellously.'

'It sounds nice,' said the Chief Fairy, whose eyes had started glittering again at the sight of the menu. 'Christine and Gavin both like crab, don't you?' They agreed, so we all ordered crab, to be followed by a plain, grilled steak, just for a change from the rich wine sauces we had been eating with our other meals.

As we waited for the food to be served I suddenly recalled another memory of my last holiday in this place. It was the first - indeed the only - time I ever saw a dog put out of a hotel for drunken behaviour.

It happened one evening when I was dining with my family. At a nearby table sat a French couple and their six-year-old son. Their dog lay obediently beneath the table. Unnoticed by the French couple, who were in animated conversation for most of the meal, their small son kept replenishing the dog's water bowl from the white wine carafe on the table. This did not seem so surprising to me at the time because I had already noticed how French families seemed to serve their children wine, too, though usually with a little water. I assumed the same applied to French dogs.

However, this turned out not to be the case, and the first that the French couple knew of their dog's condition was when it suddenly wobbled to its feet and bayed to the roof, in the way that dogs do when they hear music and they want to sing. The couple stopped talking and looked at it amazed. It then began to stagger round the restaurant, unable to put its paws down straight.

'*Regardez le chien!*' said the delighted six-year-old. '*Il danse!*' The dog wasn't actually dancing, but it looked uncommonly *like* a slow waltz. That's when the couple noticed their depleted wine carafe and the mother let loose a stream of angry French at the boy. By this time the stoned poodle was bumping into tables and chairs all over the restaurant and the boy's father had to lead it out onto the terrace and tie its leash to a table. I often wondered what sort of a head it had in the morning.

'I'm starving!' exclaimed Gavin, jerking me from my reverie of that summer long ago.

'Me, too,' said Christine, 'I wish they'd hurry up.'

'Here you are, she's coming now,' I said. I was looking forward to the meal myself, but as the waitress placed the plates in front of us a pained silence descended on the company. Crab we had ordered and, by golly, crab we had got - the whole crab, complete with shell, legs, claws and a set of nut-crackers and metal prong to tear it apart!

'What on earth's this?' Gavin groaned, glaring at it. 'I ordered crab!'

'Oh, dear,' said his mother, 'I thought it would be dressed crab.'

So did I. I picked up the nut-crackers. 'I'm afraid it's a do-it-yourself job,' I said. 'You'll have to winkle the stuff out. That's what this prong is for.'

Christine looked at hers, then drily at me. 'Oh, yes, I'll

bet they do it marvellously, you said!'

'Well, you can't win 'em all,' I replied defensively. 'Come on, let's tuck in.'

With a marked lack of enthusiasm they picked up their tools, prodded their crabs awkwardly for a moment then looked at my plate for guidance. It was not the best place to look. They watched me poking my own crab around the plate.

'Where do I start?' Gavin demanded in anguish. 'I'm starving!'

'Start with a claw and just crunch it like this,' I encouraged, suddenly taking a decision and twisting off a claw. 'See?' I crunched and they leaned forward to see how I had fared. I leaned forward too. Chunks of splintered shell were now embedded in the crab-meat.

'Oh, great!' Gavin sneered.

'Yes, well perhaps I was a bit heavy-handed there,' I said.

'Can you eat all of it?' asked Christine, going for the body instead. 'It looks a bit funny in here. Isn't there some part of a crab you're not supposed to eat?'

I had a vague feeling she was right. Or was that only when there was an M in the month - or was it R? I didn't know. 'You should be safe enough on the white meat,' I said finally.

'Actually, it's quite delicious once you get it out,' said the Chief Fairy, who seemed to be having more success. 'All you need is patience.'

And some skill, too, I thought.

Gavin's crab suddenly shot off his plate across the table and he threw his prong and nut-crackers down in disgust. 'That finishes it!' He sat back and folded his arms defiantly to indicate that a state of total deadlock now existed between him and his first course, and he for one proposed no further action to solve it.

The rest of us managed to winkle out only about a spoonful of crab-meat each, then gave up to wait for our second course. Alas, this held even less joy. Our plain grilled steaks came up with blood running from them.

'Oh, lord, they're not cooked properly,' said the Chief Fairy. 'I think we'd better send them back.'

We did, learning in the process that if you don't want your steak in that condition in France the magic words to use are '*bien cuit!*' Well done, if you please!

It was not the happiest of meals but at least we learned a couple of pitfalls to avoid in future - the French liking for under-done steaks and crabs still in their armour plating.

Our disappointment over dinner, however, was quickly forgotten in the pleasure of the tour we now made of Dinard itself. I showed them the swimming pool where I had swum as a boy, the rocks where I had played and fished from, the little ferry point with sailing boats bobbing nearby, the clean, attractive streets of little shops and cafes and the wide, sandy beach I had run and sunbathed on in that summer long ago. The children caught some of my own recollected enthusiasm and were full of questions, particularly on whether we could do the same things the next day. I said we could, if the weather was dry. The omens looked good. It was growing dark now, with a distinct chill in the air, but there was a touch of red low in the western sky which hinted at a fine day to come.

As we strolled back to our hotel, lights twinkled on the sea-front and suddenly Gavin spotted something that excited him more than anything else he'd seen that day. It was a small, promenade amusement arcade with the sound of French pop music floating from it.

'Look, Dodgems!' he exclaimed. 'Can we go on them? Please, dad!' He began to jump up and down. The lad's mad about Dodgems, so I gave him a couple of francs. 'Come on, Christine!' he shouted.

Christine hurried after him. She isn't at all crazy about Dodgems but I could see at once that the amusement centre had its attractions. There was a group of young French boys, laughing and skylarking about on them. And by the time the Chief Fairy and I strolled up they were already whistling and grinning at her in the time-honoured teenage mating ritual, which Christine pretended to treat with disdain, also in time-honoured fashion.

The Chief Fairy smiled, 'This should be interesting!'

Friendly rivalry, with much bumping, shrieking and laughing, quickly developed on the Dodgem circuit between Christine and Gavin in one car and the French boys in the others.

'I must say, she does look pretty,' said her mother proudly.

There was a sort of mass flirtation going on, with the French boys calling to her in schoolroom English as well as French, while Christine, growing pinker, answered them back in both languages. Gavin, her Dodgem chauffeur, was much more concerned with the excitement of the bumps his sister was bringing him as a bonus.

We watched the frolics with some amusement for a while then I said it was time we returned to our hotel. 'Oh, please, can't we stay - just for a little while?' pleaded Christine. 'It's great fun!'

'What - the Dodgems or the boys?' I said.

'Practising my French!' she protested.

I laughed. 'Oh, I see - that's what it is, is it?'

'Well, they're trying out their English on Gavin and me, too, aren't they, Gavin?'

'Yes,' he agreed enthusiastically. 'Please let's stay!'

Our hotel was only a short stroll away so I told them to follow on in half an hour. The reason I wanted to return was that I was beginning to feel distinctly queasy. Whether it was the assorted drinks with which I had assaulted my system in the course of the day, searching for decent loos, or whether it was mixing them with that crab, I don't know, but I could feel a touch of the Continental collywobbles coming on. A very sharp touch indeed.

By the time the kids returned I was convinced I was dying, though nobody about me seemed to care. I have noticed this before. Whenever I say I'm ill they take little notice, and the louder I groan the less notice they take. I was overcome with stomach cramps, nausea and weakness but the nearest thing I got to family concern was a cheerful, 'Why don't you lie down for a bit?' from the Chief Fairy, who promptly started to put her hair in for the night.

I lay down on the bed clutching my stomach and moaning. She went on pinning her hair up. Soon there was the sound of young voices and laughter outside the hotel and Christine and Gavin burst excitedly into the room - Christine very flushed indeed.

'Do you know what?' said Gavin. 'Eight French boys saw Christine back to the hotel!'

'Eight?' said her mother.

'It's the biggest escort I've ever had,' said a delighted Christine.

'Which one did you like best?' asked Gavin.

She shrugged. 'Oh, I don't know.'

'It was that dark-haired boy, about 15, that you were talking to most, wasn't it?' he said.

'Only because he spoke better English, but - well, he was nice, yes,' she conceded.

'There you are! Christine's got off again!' he chanted.

'Oh, shut up!' she said.

Her mother was smiling and turned to me. 'Did you hear that?

Your daughter had an escort of eight boys to see her home?'

I groaned. She could have had the whole of Dinard following her along the prom, but at that moment I couldn't have cared less. I was dying. 'I think I've been poisoned,' I said.

'Don't be silly,' said the Chief Fairy, 'you've eaten exactly the same as all of us.'

'Well, perhaps it's the whisky fighting the crab-meat,' I groaned. 'But I'm dying, I tell you!' But I was clearly in the wrong place for sympathy.

'Do you want to play cards, Christine?' said Gavin. 'We don't have to go to bed yet, do we?'

'All right,' she said. 'Do you want to play, mummy?'

'Just wait till I finish my hair,' she said.

'What about you, daddy?'

'How can I play cards when I'm dying?' I groaned.

'Do you want me to call a doctor?' said the Chief Fairy.

I looked up at her. 'Do you think you should?' I said.

'*I* don't know,' she said. 'It's up to you, isn't it? *You* know how you feel, not me.'

'He'll probably charge the earth,' I groaned. 'Here, I'll tell you what, see if they've got any stomach-settling medicine down below.'

'How do I ask for that in French?'

'I don't know, tell them I've got - got - beaucoup de nausea, and have they any Milk of Magnesia or something. Christine will help you.'

'I don't know the French for that,' Christine said.

'Well, look it up in the phrase book,' I groaned, 'there must be something in there.'

She picked up the book from the dressing table and sat on the bed. 'What would it be under?' she said, flicking over the pages. The Chief Fairy looked over her shoulder. 'There you are - General Difficulties - that should be it, shouldn't it?' she said.

Christine gave a short laugh. 'No, I don't think these are the right difficulties. Listen . . . ' she began to read the phrases aloud - '*On a vole mon sạc* - My bag has been stolen - *Cet homme suit partout* - That man is following me everywhere - *Je vais appeler un agent* - I shall call a policeman - *Au secours! Au feu! Au voleur!* - Help! Fire! Thief!'

They all began to laugh. Gavin, chanting 'Help! Fire! Thief!' jumped on the bed to join the reading over Christine's shoulder. 'Look, that's it,' he chortled, pointing. 'Popular Idioms. That's daddy's case, look! *C'est tordant, c'est rigolo* - it's terribly funny - *Vous vous moquez de moi* - you're pulling my leg - *vous exagerez* - you exaggerate! - *Doucement* - Take it easy!'

He began to roll about the bed. 'Oh, that's the French for daddy's case all right - *vous exagerez* - you exaggerate!'

This hilarity was doing nothing for my weakened condition. 'Look under illness, you fools,' I groaned.

'Oh, sorry, yes, there it is,' said the Chief Fairy, suddenly pointing at a page. 'How do you say that in French, Christine?'

'*Avez-vous un remède pour le mal d'estomac?* Have you a remedy for stomach-ache?'

'That'll do,' I said. 'Go and ask for that. And for God's sake stop jumping up and down on the bed Gavin, will you? I'm wobbling enough inside!'

Ten minutes later they came back with a bottle of white liquid and a spoon, borrowed from the proprietor's wife. 'Two teaspoonfuls of that should do the trick,' said the Chief Fairy, offering me a spoonful of the liquid. It tasted foul.

'Now can we get on with the game of cards?' said Gavin, and promptly began to deal them on the end of my death-bed.

Why can't I ever be ill with anxious faces and ministering hands and words of comfort about me? Why does everybody assume that I'm just a hypochondriac?

9 It's Calamity Chain

The borrowed medicine must have done the trick because next morning I awoke feeling much better, though still a little weak. I was also a trifle disturbed by the memory of a nightmare during my fevered hours, which had obviously been conjured from emotional highspots of the day.

I had attended my own funeral, seeing my body committed to a watery grave from the high diving board of Dinard open air swimming pool. The cortege drove up in Dodgems and as the Union Jack-draped coffin slid into the water, Navy-style, from a tilted top board, my family stood around the water's edge wearing pained expressions - pained because they were all bursting to go to the loo.

Such is the stuff of dreams.

But I was awake now and all that was gone. The sun was streaming through the balcony windows and I was feeling hungry for some croissants and coffee. 'So,' said the Chief Fairy, as I tucked into them, 'dying were you? I see little sign of *rigor mortis*.'

'Well, that's what it felt like,' I muttered.

'I told you *vous exagerez!*' chortled Gavin.

We spent the morning on the beach and at the pool, and by mid-day I was back to my old self again. Instead of our usual daily picnic we lunched at a little sea-front restaurant on the most delicious sweet and savoury pancakes I have ever tasted.

The pancake is a speciality of Brittany and how mouth-wateringly the cafés and restaurants pursue it.

This was the day I saw the Chief Fairy let out the first notch in the belt of her pretty summer dress. She grimaced guiltily. 'Another couple of lunches like that,' she said, 'and I'll have to switch into my going home dresses. But how can you resist pancakes like that? Weren't they gorgeous?'

'Why resist?' I said. 'We're on holiday.'

I had planned to motor on round Brittany after lunch but under pressure from Christine and Gavin we stayed one more night in Dinard. They wanted to go on the Dodgems again. They had already had a ride when we came up from the beach, but the boys of the night before weren't there. They still weren't there when Christine and Gavin returned in the evening with their Dodgem francs clutched in their hands. Christine looked downcast. 'Never mind,' I said, 'we might call back on our journey home.'

'Oh, could we?' she exclaimed, brightening.

'Sure - and you can practise your French again.'

She pulled a face at me, but looked much happier.

Two days later we were 300 miles south, heading through Western France for the Dordogne, and one thing was becoming imperatively clear: we had to start economising on our francs. We had wildly overshot the daily allowance I had set for ourselves. This was my fault. I had been totally carried away by the charm of Brittany and whenever we stopped to eat or put up at an hotel for the night it seemed a shame to spoil it by stinting ourselves. We had wined and dined and lunched on the best - and the best in France is unbeatable anywhere in the world.

But one could see at once why Brittany, France's most westerly province, was so popular among Britons fleeing from their own chilly shores. The warm waters of the Gulf Stream which lap its friendly shores produce an outstandingly mild climate, and Spring comes early. Through almost every little village and picturesque fishing port we passed through, mimosas, hydrangeas and roses were bursting in profusion.

We had no time to tour Brittany's full 800-mile coastline but we saw enough to be very impressed - sweeping bays, with intimate coves and fine sandy beaches. Then we motored leisurely through the hinterland of moors and forests, short tidal rivers and historic cities, and once we got caught up in a spring festival where the village was decorated for the fete. And a splendid sight it made in the spring sunshine.

The kids got out of the car to take some pictures but the Chief Fairy remained pensively in her seat. I don't think she'd quite recovered from a fright she'd had the night before at one of our overnight stops, an old inn.

It had been late at night when we arrived there after searching unsuccessfully for two hours down darkening country lanes. Suddenly the old inn stood out starkly, silhouetted against the skyline. Inside, we had no trouble booking for the night, but as we did so the Chief Fairy glanced about her apprehensively.

'What's wrong?' I said.

'Bit sort of - spooky, isn't it?' she muttered.

'That's just because it's old,' I said. 'It's all fairly old in these parts of Brittany.'

But she was right. The place certainly had an atmosphere. It wasn't just the old beams, wooden floors and heavy timber doors with solid iron locks, there was an air of brooding decay about the place. Nor was it helped by the poor lighting over the entrance hall and staircase.

'I don't see any other guests,' she muttered, still looking about her.

'Well, it is out of season,' I said, 'and I suppose we are off the beaten track a bit.'

But she was still uneasy. As we were led up the winding staircase by a thin, and what seemed in the half-light, sepulchral-faced Frenchman, distant creaks and sighing winds emanated from the shadows.

'You don't think it's haunted, do you?' whispered Christine nervously, now infected by her mother's uneasiness.

'Rubbish!' I retorted.

Suddenly, on the dim landing, Gavin pulled his anorak over his head, stretched out his arms and made a low, wailing sound behind her. She shrieked. 'Gavin, don't you dare do that! Daddy, stop him!'

'Cut it out!' I ordered. 'Now everybody get some sleep because we've got a long day of travelling tomorrow.'

It seemed that I had just fallen asleep when I was prodded awake by the Chief Fairy. 'What's that?' she hissed urgently in my ear.

I came drowsily out of my slumber, and groaned. She's a great one for cutting me in on things in the middle of the night. She does it with thunderstorms, too, just in case I should sleep through them.

'What's what?' I muttered.

'That weird cackling! I've been listening to it for ages - it's coming from outside our bedroom window! Listen, there it is again!'

A strange, wobbling cackle rose in the half-light outside the window, then as quickly died away again. It was certainly unnerving to an ear still half asleep. The Chief Fairy pulled herself closer to me. 'Oh, God, what do you think it is?' she said anxiously.

'Ssh, let me hear it again,' I said.

Shades of *Jane Eyre* and mad women locked in dark country attics had clearly filled her mind while she'd been listening to it. 'I think it's a mad woman who's escaped from somewhere,' she whispered.

'Ssh, let me hear it properly,' I said. We lay in silence for a few moments then suddenly it rose again - and this time I recognised it at once. 'For heaven's sake,' I said, 'have you woken me up just to listen to a bubblyjock?'

'A what?' she said.

'A bubblyjock - a turkey! You've heard one before, haven't you? That's the sound they make - bubblyjock-bubblyjock!' I imitated the turkey call to demonstrate the point and at once an answering call came back from outside the window.

'A turkey!' she repeated, amazed.

'Yes! Not a mad woman in an attic - a turkey! Now go to

sleep, will you? We've a busy day tomorrow.'

'Well, good lord, fancy that!' she said. I went back to sleep.

But now we were near Limoges, deep in South West France, and needing another bed for the night. We had come that day along the beautiful banks of the Loire and seen the chateaux and the wine groves and had marvelled at it all. We had also seen on the banks of the same beautiful river, in an old-world village of great charm, the very nadir of public conveniences, positioned on the side of the road and overlooking the river. It was, said Gavin, with horror, 'the stinkingest, foulest loo I've ever seen.' And by now he was something of an expert on French loos.

Once again we paid over our coffee and Coke money to use a wayside restaurant's facilities, but this time it was a ploy that was to end in a small calamity.

We had pulled up at an olde-worlde, touristy place, full of red plush and antique bric-a-brac. While the Chief Fairy and Christine settled down to their coffee and Coke, Gavin and I went in search of the loo. We were looking round upstairs when Gavin suddenly said, 'Cor, this is better - look at this!'

He was standing at the entrance to a small, curtained room off the landing. Inside was the most attractive lavatory I've ever seen. It was small but beautifully shaped in porcelain and decorated with coloured designs and in complete contrast to the other horrors we'd been fleeing from. Over it hung what looked like a pearl-handled chain. We were delighted with it. Near it was a period table, chair and footstool. Here, at last, was a place with more than civilised standards. It had obviously been put in by a Frenchman with a conscience and an eye for the tourists. The only snag seemed to be that there were curtains instead of a door, though even this, we both agreed, was an improvement on some of the open-plan public loos we'd used.

'Go ahead,' I said to Gavin. 'I'll wait here on the landing and keep guard.'

I heard him splashing away but a moment or two later he came out frowning. 'I can't pull the chain,' he said. 'It's stuck.'

'Okay, I'll do it,' I said. 'You keep guard here while I have a run-off.'

As I did so I found myself gazing at the beautifully wrought, intricate designs on the cistern. It was a work of real craftsmanship, and I found my heart warming to its designer. There was no reason at all why a strictly utilitarian piece of equipment should not be made attractive also.

Having attended to the pressing matter of nature, I reached for the pearl-handled chain and pulled it. Nothing happened, Gavin was right, it had stuck. I pulled again - harder - but it was locked solid. The ballcock had obviously jammed, so I pulled the footstool out and stood on it to look into the cistern.

Horror of horrors! The reason it wouldn't flush was that it was filled with geraniums!

Too late I realised the whole thing was an ornament, a miniature period piece for show. The velvet curtains, the period furniture, the whole set-up now fell into place. I looked down into the lavatory basin - it was draining away, but God knows where!

I stepped quickly off the stool and hustled Gavin downstairs. 'Quick,' I said to the others at the table, 'we're leaving.'

'But I haven't finished my coffee yet,' said the Chief Fairy.

'Never mind your coffee,' I said. 'Let's get out of here before the ceiling starts leaking!'

Apart from that, the day had gone well. That is, if we overlook the total confusion in trying to find our way out of Rennes to Angers. Due to the lack of French signposting we finished up in the middle of a city housing estate - though this in part may have been due to the Chief Fairy's navigation.

But our spirits quickly bounced up again once we were on the open road heading south towards the city of Limoges.

'What we must look out for tonight,' I said, 'is a nice cheap place. The francs are running low.'

We decided to by-pass Limoges in the hope of finding a small

inn on the country roads. Dusk was falling now and all the family had their eyes peeled for a likely spot.

Some 12 miles south of the city and in pretty, wooded countryside, the Chief Fairy suddenly pointed, 'Oh, that looks nice!'

Set back from the road was an old, rambling inn. It looked perfect, a real rural haven. Creepers climbed the trellis on the white-washed walls and warm lights gleamed behind the small, leaded windows. A sign 'Hotel-Restaurant' hung over the door and without hesitation I pulled the car into the cobbled courtyard in front of it.

'Stay here and I'll check,' I said, 'just in case they can't put us up.'

'I hope they can,' said Christine, 'it looks *very* cosy, doesn't it? Just like something in a picture postcard.'

It did too. Inside it was even cosier, with low, black beams and a fire burning in an inglenook-type fireplace. I put the building about the 16th century, probably an old coaching house, and though a few modernisation essentials had been incorporated for comfort, the atmosphere had been kept. There was a warm, nostalgic friendliness about it and the more I glanced round the more I hoped they would have room for us here. Inside the low entrance hall I had seen the day's menu in a glass frame on the wall, and I was delighted to note that among its obvious pleasures was a 15 franc tourist dinner - four courses that looked as though they would have the Chief Fairy's mouth watering in no time.

'*M'sieu?*' A slim, dark-haired Frenchman came through the door, which obviously led to the kitchens. He was wearing a chef's apron.

'Ah, *bonsoir, m'sieu,*' I replied and asked if he had a large room for the night, to accommodate my family.

'*Oui, m'sieu,*' he smiled, and checked in the register on the heavy wooden counter that served as a reception desk. '*Numero trois.*'

'Could I see it?'

'*Mais oui, m'sieu.*' He called a passing waitress to show me to it. The room was ideal, large, simply furnished with two capacious double beds and a screened wash-hand basin. On the back of the door, as is obligatory in all French hotels, was the daily charge - 17 francs. It was a marvellous bargain after our extravagances of previous nights in 50, 60 and 70 franc rooms. Now all of us could sleep in comfort in this charming old world inn for a little less than 30 bob. The family were delighted with it, and once we were installed and cleaned up we trooped down to dinner in the candle-lit restaurant. Here we were in for an even more delightful surprise. The walls were covered with good food diplomas, prizes and guide recommendations.

'And a 15 franc menu,' I said. 'What a find!'

We ordered the tourist menu, then the waiter brought us the hand-written wine list. What a selection! Some of the bottles went up to 300 francs, £25. Of course such extravagance was out of the question. However, we were weary after our long journey and I felt that since we were making such wonderful economies with the room and the tourist dinner we could splash out on a bottle of something pleasant.

It was then that my eye lit on a superb *Chevalier Montrachet* at only 27 francs (about £2.25). A fantastic bargain! No wonder the hotel walls were plastered with prizes. I had dipped my tonsils in that particular juice before, so I knew all about it. I promptly ordered a bottle and was pleased to note that the wine waiter's face brightened with what seemed surprise and pleasure. Here, obviously, was an Englishman with a discerning palate and an eye for a bargain.

In fact, it seemed that he couldn't quite believe his own ears. He leaned forward deferentially to repeat and confirm my order. '*Chevalier Montrachet, m'sieu?*' he said, pointing to the item on the wine list.

'*Oui, bon,* you bet,' I said. 'And if you don't mind could we have it now while we're waiting for the starters? We're a bit thirsty after a hard day on the road.'

'*Oui, m'sieu. Tout de suite.*' He moved off bowing. In fact, it seemed that he was almost backing away with reverence as though from a kingly presence, which is certainly something he hadn't been doing for any other diners.

Here I must make a small confession. I do like impressing

French wine waiters - though, of course, like 99 per cent of us wine-bibers, I really don't know that much about it. Oh, sure, yes, I enjoy the phonus bolonus that goes with the tasting - dipping the lips into the claret and musing, 'Ah, an impertinent little fellow. Quite audacious.' I particularly love sipping a Burgundy and launching into all that erotic imagery about 'buxom, full-bodied, flirtatious reds,' (I am still on wines, by the way, not Communist sex-pots) but I certainly wouldn't claim to be an expert. Which, however, is not to say that I can't give a very good impression of one - flicking a seemingly practised eye down a wine list, hoisting the critical eyebrow at the right moment, then despatching the waiter with my order. The only matter that remains totally in doubt is what the upshot will be.

In this case the waiter had been very impressed indeed. When he returned he was carrying the wine in a champagne bucket of ice on a silver stand. He began to twirl the bottle gently in the ice while singing its praises. '*C'est magnifique, m'sieu, Chevalier Montrachet, oui?*'

'*Oui*,' I said. It seemed to me that he was fluttering about and making even more of a fuss over it than when I ordered it - so much fuss, in fact, that I wasn't getting my tonsils into it. He wouldn't let me taste it.

'*Non, non, m'sieu*,' he said, then broke into pidgin English. 'Ze temperature ees not quite right. We wait *un peu, oui?*'

So we waited *un peu* to please him since he seemed to be saying all the right things, and my family were suitably impressed at a father with such *savoir faire*. But after he had passed our table two or three times while my throat grew drier, I said to him, 'Look, couldn't we let it out now?'

He frowned. 'Let it out, *m'sieu?*'

'Let it out of the bottle - the wine. Let it escape. Pour it.'

He shrugged, then almost grudgingly poured me a sample. My lips rolled round it. There was no need for the nonsense about it being an elegant wine, or a humorous one, or a friendly one. There was only one word for it. Sensational.

'Oh, just wait till you taste that!' I said triumphantly.

'Can I have some, too?' said Gavin. 'I like white wine.'

'You should be on Coke or lemonade,' I said, 'but never mind, this is so special we'll put it down to your education. You should learn early what a great wine tastes like - and you don't have to pay the earth for it if you know your way around a wine list.'

Could God let me get away with such smug boasting?

'Please can I taste it?' said Christine. So we all got at it. The waiter poured liberal measures all round.

'Oh, lordy,' said the Chief Fairy, 'I don't know whether it's because I'm in the mood for a glass of wine or it's the wine itself but isn't it absolutely delicious? It's gone straight to my toes.'

It went to my toes, too. It went to everybody's toes. It slipped down like chilled liquid velvet, and was gone before the second course arrived.

'What about another bottle?' I said.

'Do you think we should?' said the Chief Fairy. 'You said we must economise.'

'We have economised,' I said. 'Seventeen francs for a room for all of us and twenty-five bob for a meal like this? That wine is a superb bargain as well.'

'Well, if you think it's all right, I'm not going to resist it!' she giggled. 'I must say it's gorgeous.'

So I hailed the wine waiter again. '*Une autre bouteille, s'il vous plaît?*'

His eyebrows rose. 'Anuzzer bottle, *m'sieu?*'

'*Oui, bon. Ce n'est pas magnifique, c'est fantastique!*' I grinned amiably.

'*Oui, m'sieu, c'est fantastique, vraiment.*'

He moved off to bring the second bottle and I turned to the Chief Fairy. 'There you are, I told him it wasn't only magnificent it was fantastic and he agreed, it's truly fantastic.'

So we both polished off the second bottle with the delicious *brochette maison* that came with the tourist dinner.

Needless to say we slept like babes that night and next morning rose to a day of brilliant sunshine and the sounds of the country outside the open window. I stood at the window listening to the spring-happy birds and gulping in great draughts of country air. I could feel that it was going to be a perfect day.

'Tell you what,' I said, 'I've been looking at the map and I see we're not far from Rocamadour. It's quite a tourist attraction, a remarkable ancient city, the oldest in Medieval France, I believe, and still preserved. It's perched on the side of a sheer mountain right in the heart of the country. We could have a look at that today.'

'That would be nice,' said the Chief Fairy.

'Why is it built on the side of a mountain?' asked Gavin.

'That's how they used to build them in ancient times around a castle so they could defend them better against attackers,' I said.

'Oh, I'd like to see that,' he said enthusiastically. 'I could write about that, couldn't I?'

'Perfect,' I said with a grin, 'for your holiday essay.' So the matter was agreed. 'And if we can find another inn like this one for the night we'll be laughing. Then maybe tomorrow we might push on south into Spain.'

As we sat over breakfast, happily contemplating the day ahead, I noted with pleasure that the croissants and coffee were only five francs - the cheapest breakfast we'd had so far. Truly this old country inn was a marvellous find, and when the innkeeper, the dark-haired Frenchman in the chef's apron of the night before - he apparently supervised all the cooking, too - came into the little dining room, I congratulated him.

'*Merci, m'sieu,*' he smiled. He was pleased, he said, that we had enjoyed ourselves. And had we liked the wine?

'Only fantastic,' I said.

He smiled again. '*Bon!*'

We were now ready to leave and I asked him if he would be kind enough to bring me the bill. '*L'addition? Oui, m'sieu.*' He already had it with him and he handed it to me. I nearly collapsed.

The bill was nearly treble what I had expected, £25.

For a moment I stared at the total - 297 francs - then with sudden understanding I recovered and said, 'Ah, yes, I think you've made a mistake, *m'sieu.* You have given me somebody else's bill.'

He frowned. '*Non, m'sieu.* Room numbair three.' He leaned over my shoulder and we examined it together, me with a panic-stricken eye running down the scrawled items. Room, 17 francs, yes. Dinner, 15 francs each, yes. Breakfast, 5 francs each, yes. Then wine - 194 francs.

'What!' I ejaculated. 'A hundred and ninety-four francs for wine! That can't be right. The bottles were 27 francs each.'

'*Non, m'sieu.*' he said. '*Un moment.*' And he went to bring me the wine list. While he was fetching it I groaned, 'God, I hope it is a mistake. It's got to be a mistake - I haven't enough francs to pay for it.'

'What'll we do?' said Gavin anxiously. 'Will we have to wash the dishes or something?'

'Don't be silly,' said Christine. 'That just happens in films, doesn't it, daddy?'

They all turned to look at me. 'Of course it does,' I said quickly. 'That's just Laurel and Hardy stuff - oh, don't worry. Of course there's been a mistake. Look, here he comes now.'

The innkeeper handed me the wine list. '*Voilà, m'sieu.*' He pointed down the hand-written list. '*Chevalier Montrachet* - 97 francs.' I stared in horror. It was indeed 97 francs, not 27. It was that crazy French writing full of curls, swoops and unfinished loops that had fooled me. Like the menu, the wine list was scrawled on lined paper and in the candlelit restaurant I'd mistaken the line under the ill-completed '9' as the base of a '2'.

No wonder the wine waiter had been impressed. No wonder he had fluttered over the bottle and bowed and scraped around me. No wonder he had agreed it was fantastic when I ordered a second bottle. What sort of lunatic puts up in a 17 franc room, orders the cut-price menu and two bottles of wine at £8 a bottle?

'Ees right, *m'sieu? Oui?*' said the innkeeper.

'*Oui,*' I said, a bit hoarsely, and looked slowly up at him. How was I going to break the news? He wasn't smiling now.

10 Pay Up or Wash Up!

For sheer embarrassment I can think of few experiences to match that moment when, having dined well, wined well and beamed expansively on the bowing waiter, you call for the bill and find you can't pay it.

The mind goes numb with despair. Wild schemes of escape begin to burgeon. Suppose . . . suppose we were all to pretend to go to the loo, one by one, then sneak out of the back door and jump into the car? No! The car's parked smack in front of the dining room. He'd spot us all before we could escape. If he didn't actually catch us he'd alert the police with our car number and we'd have gendarmes chasing us all round the Dordogne. No, forget it - impossible!

In any case, the innkeeper had now withdrawn to his reception desk where he was hovering, watching us suspiciously, waiting to be called for payment. Escape was out.

Desperately, I plunged my hand into my back pocket, withdrew my wad of franc notes, then emptied my pockets of all small change. The family leaned forward, watching me as I counted. I'd got exactly 243 francs, 20 centimes - and the bill was 297 francs.

I looked at the faces around me. There was nothing for it but to have a whip-round of all available pockets and handbags to see how close we could get to the total.

'How much has everybody got?' I whispered.

Gavin at once stuck his toes in. 'You're not pinching *my*

money!' he said, pulling back sharply from his examination of mine.

'I've got to pay the bill!' I hissed. 'I need all the francs I can get!'

The Chief Fairy was already emptying her purse - 'I've got 18 francs and 70 centimes here,' she said.

'Come on, Gavin!' scolded Christine. 'We've all got to help!' She turned out 7 francs 40 centimes from her own purse. 'Or do you want to wash the dishes?'

'Oh, blimey!' he groaned and reluctantly stuck his hand in his pocket. 'That's 5 francs 40 centimes you owe me and I want it back!'

'You'll get it back,' I muttered, nervously adding it all up.

There was a total of 264 francs 55 centimes, which was about £4 short (33 francs 45 centimes). We had no English money left, but what I hoped was that the innkeeper would let me make up the balance from our ration of Spanish pesetas, which we weren't supposed to start dipping into for two days yet.

The vital question was: would he accept pesetas instead of francs? Glancing furtively at him, I had the feeling that he would greet it with the same enthusiasm as if I offered him Chinese yen. We were deep in the heart of the country, and it was a bit like tendering francs to pay a pub bill to a Scotsman in the Highlands.

I was about to rise from the table and put the matter to the test when there was a 'miaow' at my feet and Gavin exclaimed, 'Look, a cat just like Smokey!' I looked down. He was right. It was a grey Persian with a white bib, but a second's scrutiny was enough to establish it wasn't Smokey. Anyway, Smokey was 800 miles away, incarcerated in her cats' holiday home, but the momentary interruption was sufficient to freeze me back in my seat.

The cat was staring up at me with a look of reproof - the same look that had been on Smokey's face when I had bundled her into the cats' home. All right, put it down to my nervousness and unstable imagination, but for a split second I wondered if this was Smokey's prophecy coming home to roost. Had she in some strange, telepathic way communicated with this animal at my feet and instructed it to pass on the message: 'I told you no good would come of all this.'

An involuntary shiver ran through me. Who knows what can go on in the cat world? I rose quickly to deal with the innkeeper.

'Ah, *m'sieu,*' I said, clutching my francs in one hand and my pesetas in the other. 'I have a slight problem here.'

He said nothing but the frown on his face said plenty. Burbling a bit now, I explained my problem - or rather, our mutual problem - and my plan for solving it.

'Pesetas?' he muttered and looked at the three pounds worth in my hand as though they were some kind of dreaded fungus. He shook his head slowly. '*Non.*' I noticed that he'd dropped the '*m'sieu*'.

After a moment he looked up and said, 'Traveller's cheque?'

'I'm afraid not,' I said. 'We just brought francs and pesetas, but perhaps if you could cash an English cheque?' I pulled out my cheque book but he shrank away as if it were an even deadlier fungus. '*Non, non,*' he muttered, shaking his head again.

It looked like deadlock. With a total lack of enthusiasm he began to count out my francs on his counter.

'Miaow!' The cat was at my feet again, looking up at me. I stared back at it and just for a second found myself trying desperately to communicate through its eyes to Smokey. Crazy, I know, but the thought flashed through my mind, 'For God's sake, Smokey, if you've got anything to do with this at all, please rescue us now! I promise I'll be kinder!'

Suddenly - and grudgingly - the innkeeper said, 'All right, I take ze pesetas.'

'Oh, thank you!' I breathed, handing them over quickly, and we all sped out.

'Who's a great big steaming nit then? Eh? Who wants his marbles examined? To say nothing of his eyesight?'

It was Gavin at his most scathing. The tones were dry and biting, and when that boy whips out his rapier of critical scorn no second-former thrusts it home with more painful dexterity.

The fact that it was his own father who was the target did not - indeed, never does - deter him or blunt his rapier point. If anything it sharpens it.

The days when children were seen and not heard are long gone. In all conscience I cannot mourn them, but I sometimes wonder about the new order in which they, like their mothers, are all apparently equal - merely occupying different roles in our new enlightened society.

'You mustn't speak to your father like that,' the Chief Fairy said sternly, in a valiant attempt to re-establish something of the old order.

'But he's pinched all my pocket money!' he protested hotly. 'And Christine's too! *And* yours!'

'All right, all right,' I muttered. 'I told you I'd pay you back when I can get hold of some more francs.'

'When's that going to be?' he snorted. 'Suppose I see something I want to buy *now*! I can't even buy any crisps!' For him calamities don't come much greater than that.

At this time we were climbing into the car outside our charming, olde worlde, 'economical' hotel, in considerably gloomier mood than when we'd arrived down to breakfast. The sun was still shining, the birds still singing and the spring air warm on our faces, but a chilly dampness - which I sincerely hoped was temporary - lay upon our spirits.

As the car doors slammed shut and I started up the engine, Gavin made a final thrust from the back seat. 'Oh, that wine, a superb bargain, old boy,' he mimicked drily. 'Learn your way round a wine list, son, and you too can have bargains like that!'

I caught the flicker of a smile at the Chief Fairy's lips as she gazed ahead out of the window, but it vanished as quickly as it came, and she said sharply; 'Be quiet now! I don't want to hear any more from you on the subject!'

We drove on in silence for a while then my conscience got at me, as it usually does, I find, when I'm dealing with children. 'I suppose the lad's right,' I said. 'I dropped a real clanger there.'

It's nice to dream of the authoritarian, revered father figure, whose judgement isn't questioned and who is regarded as the fount of all knowledge, but it's only a dream. It cannot be based on reality when father is as fallible and occasionally as cloth-headed as the next man. Certainly, any hopes I had entertained that our journey across France might produce some of that filial subservience and admiration characterised in the Dupont and Duval families of those French primers - '*Oui, papa, non, papa, ici vos* slippers, *papa*' - had now vanished, and I suppose with good cause.

Each day my children had observed me at close quarters in my various roles as a shoulder-shrugging French linguist, loo finder, expert in right-handed traffic, interpreter of menus, virtuoso of the duet for nutcrackers and crabs - and now as a wine-list connoisseur. What could survive after that? And there was still more than half the holiday to come.

'The fact is,' I said, 'any real wine expert wouldn't have believed that price on the menu. He'd have questioned it and not dropped into the pitfall I fell into. I confess it.'

'It was a natural enough mistake,' consoled the Chief Fairy. 'I must say I had to look twice at it before I realised it was a 9 not a 2.'

'Well,' I said, trying to look on the bright side, 'at least we didn't finish up washing dishes.' Though how close we came to it I'll never know. There was certainly a moment when those Laurel and Hardy scenes which I had so confidently pooh-poohed flashed across my mind, with all of us in the hotel kitchen, our sleeves up and nose-high in dishes. A small shudder sped through me as I speculated on what Gavin's reactions would have been then - never mind requisitioning his pocket money to help us out of the crisis.

We were now totally cleaned out of francs but I felt sure that I would be able to cash an English cheque at a bank in the next big town, Uzerche or Brives, which lay on our route south. Luckily I had filled up the petrol tank before our overnight stop so that raised no problem. But I was kicking myself for not bringing travellers' cheques instead of pesetas.

I had confidently expected that the franc allowance I had equipped ourselves with would last us for ten days. Now, six days later, it had all gone, leaving us only with our peseta ration for four days in Spain. And we still had to return through France to get home. Some cheap holiday!

There's no doubt that France is one great country for the tourist, but fiercely expensive, and you need an iron will to resist the temptations to overspend on food and wine. Without that iron will, you land in the sort of pickle we had landed in.

Nor, I must say at once, had we reached the bottom of our own pickle jar. As we approached Uzerche, 60 kilometres south, I had the feeling that something was not quite right. It had been growing on me for some time but I hadn't yet put my finger on it; I had been too preoccupied with reflections on the scenery around us as our road wound through the undulating and picturesque Department of Coreze. The villages we had come through had seemed oddly quiet, but I had put it down to the fact that we were touring out of season, but now on the outskirts of Uzerche the answer suddenly came to me. The reason why everything was quiet was that it was Sunday! No banks open!

'Oh, dear, what shall we do?' said the Chief Fairy anxiously.

'We'll just have to press on and try to reach Spain by tonight. It's about 300 miles,' I said, 'but at least I've got their currency and it must be cheaper.' This, as far as I was concerned, was now the prime consideration. I was sure, if it came to the push, we could do something with our pesetas somewhere, as far as food and drink went, but I was now more concerned about the need for economy.

'What about Rocamadour?' demanded Gavin, in the back seat. 'You said we could go and see the mountain city!'

'Maybe some other time,' I said.

'No! Not some other time - now! You promised! You said I could write about it in my essay.'

Foolish is the man who makes promises to children. He should say nothing and let everything come as a surprise - or not.

The Chief Fairy saw me hesitating, in doubt. 'If you think we should go on, let's go on,' she said.

'Well, I suppose it's not too far off our route. We could take a flier on it. If the worst comes to the worst tonight, we'll kip in the car.'

'It's up to you, dear,' she said, 'you know best.' She said it casually, then frowned. I recalled the last time she had used a similar phrase was when I'd ordered the second £8 bottle of wine.

I shrugged. Okay, what-the-heck! Research costs on this holiday essay had already shot through the roof anyway. 'Right, the mountain city it is,' I said.

'Great!' said Gavin.

11 And So to Tent . . .

It is easy to see why the province of Dordogne, with its forest-fringed rivers winding through valleys of sometimes spectacular beauty, has emerged from relative obscurity to become a star tourist attraction. One wonders only how it could ever have been passed by in the first place. It is at once a province of peace and charm. Rich landscapes, wooded hills and quiet country lanes unfold before the motorist, and high above the rivers and villages sit splendid mediaeval castles sharing the exquisite views that delight the tourist from almost every hill top.

The Dordogne, long steeped in violent history, has grown warm and gentle with the ageing. It is a paradise for the gourmet and the sightseer. The mediaeval towns, such as Périgueux, Cahors and Sarlat are still beautifully preserved, as are also the prehistoric caves with their wall paintings and drawings that abound in the area. Excellent little hotels, riverside inns and restaurants beckon the traveller at almost every beauty spot - but in our case, of course, we ignored them. We were on bread and cheese for lunch.

What's more, it was yesterday's bread and cheese, left over from our daily picnic.

'Some Sunday dinner!' grumbled Gavin, chewing his ration by the roadside. We had stopped just outside Rocamadour for our *al fresco* lunch.

'We'll eat a proper meal later,' I said, crossing my fingers.

However, his discontent quickly vanished in his enthusiasm for this strange and ancient city, perched with its castle on the side of a precipitous hill, with country roads winding in the valley below.

'What a fantastic place!' he breathed as we topped a hill at the end of the valley and saw it in the distance. 'All the houses seem to be standing on top of each other!'

'As I told you, that was to make it difficult, if not impossible, for any marauders to attack from the valley below,' I said. 'It's got quite a history.' You could feel it, too, as you walked through the narrow, cobbled streets, lined by little souvenir shops. We were so fascinated by the place that it was nearly three hours before we finished our tour and returned to the car. We had wandered everywhere in the warm spring sun, taking pictures at points of interest, window-shopping in the souvenir boutiques and reading the legends of this strange old place that had slumbered so long in the tourist shade.

It was now late in the afternoon and I knew we could never reach the Spanish border that night. I wasn't even going to try. We'd just have to take pot luck with our pesetas. But I didn't want to leave it too late. Neither did Gavin.

'I'm hungry,' he protested after we'd been driving for an hour.

'I'm not only hungry, I'm starving!' said Christine. 'Do you realise all we've eaten today is croissants for breakfast and bread and cheese for lunch?'

'Stale bread and cheese!' corrected Gavin.

'Don't knock it,' I said. 'There are many hungry children in this world who would be delighted to lunch on stale bread and cheese.'

Gavin groaned, 'Oh, not that again! Name one then! Go on!' He burst into laughter. 'There you are, you can't, can you! But you're always saying it!'

'That's no argument,' I said, but he was determined to press home his advantage. He was enjoying himself.

'The only reason we're all on bread and cheese is because we're still paying for all that wine you guzzled!' He rocked back in his seat, laughing again. There are no flies on today's kids. They see it all, and I began to pine for the old family order.

Happily, I wasn't required to continue this uneven contest because at that moment I suddenly spied what I had been looking for. We had been motoring leisurely along empty country roads over hills and into valleys when, quite suddenly, we rounded a bend on the outskirts of a village and came upon an old grey-stone building with the sign 'Restaurant-Bar' hanging outside.

'Let's try here,' I said, pulling the car up outside. They all piled out to follow me.

The restaurant was set back among trees, with fields rising behind and a stream flowing in front of it. It was a pretty setting. I pushed open the restaurant door. Inside it was almost empty. A couple of men, whom I took to be locals, sat at the bar watching a TV set flickering in a darkened corner. Clark Gable was performing in an old movie and speaking immaculate French.

A plump, cheerful-faced woman in her forties moved out of the bar to greet us. '*Bon soir, m'sieu!*'

I said 'good evening' back and explained my problem. We had run out of francs but we had pesetas. Would she permit us to pay for a meal in pesetas?

'*Certainement!*' she smiled.

'Oh, good!' said Christine, and though the Chief Fairy said nothing I felt her sigh of relief beside me. She too had had nothing but stale bread and cheese for lunch.

The menu looked good - and cheap. The thought occurred to me that since *Madame* had made no fuss about taking pesetas it might be a good place to stop the night. But, alas, she regretted she had no accommodation. It was just a bar and restaurant.

Gavin, who had been drawn to the TV set - as he always is, like a moth to a light - marvelled at the French spoken by Clark Gable.

'That's not him, it's been dubbed, you idiot!' said Christine.

'Well, it's very good just the same,' he said.

While we were looking at the menu Gavin went out to the back for his customary loo inspection, and a little while later came back, his face bright with enthusiasm. 'Here,' he said, 'there's camping in the field behind. It says on a notice "*Le Camping*." Why don't we sleep in the tent?'

The idea fell on deaf ears, as so many of his ideas do.

Nobody said anything. We just carried on reading the menu.

'Well, at least it would be cheap!' he said to me. 'It says it's one franc for the night to put a tent up.'

His concern for my dwindling finances would have been quite touching except for the fact that I knew he couldn't care less about it. All he was concerned about was sleeping in a tent. But he knew the chink in my armour and I found myself thinking about it.

We had the tent in the car for emergencies. Well, was this an emergency? Yes. By the time we finished our meal dusk would be falling and perhaps we might not so easily find another place that would take pesetas.

I voiced my thoughts. 'What do you think?' I said to the Chief Fairy. 'We've got a ground sheet and some blankets and the rug in the car.'

'Be a bit boney, won't it?' she said.

'No, it won't,' said Gavin. 'There's a whole load of hay in a barn out there. We could put it under the ground sheet! It'd be great!'

She looked at him doubtfully, then at Christine. 'I'm game,' said Christine. 'It might be fun.'

Sensing victory for his project, Gavin got more excited. 'Dad and I could put the tent up while you wait here and then we could all sit and watch the telly till it's time to go to bed! Just like home!'

That was the clincher. 'All right,' said his mother. 'We'll try it if you like.'

The matter was agreed. It turned out that the field was owned by the restaurant and after our meal - in which I left the wine list strictly alone - I paid *Madame* one franc for our night's lodging. Gavin and I then collected the tent, ground sheet and blankets from the car and went into the field at the back to choose a suitable site.

It had been many, many years since I last camped, a truth which would have been quickly evident to any onlooker watching me put the tent up. But the only audience my efforts had were two cows, chewing the cud and looking at me mournfully - or it could have been derisively.

Matters were not helped by the fact that a wind had sprung up and guy ropes and canvas kept flying all over the place as I tried to fit the poles into the right holes. After several failures, with Gavin holding one end and me trying to pin down the other end, he grew a little exasperated. 'Look, you don't know anything about it, do you?' he said. 'Let me do it! You hold this pole and we'll do one end at a time. We'll start with mine.'

At last we got it up and the tent pegs pushed in firmly. 'Now let's get the hay from over there,' he said. I wondered whether we should. 'Well, we can put it back in the morning, can't we?' he said.

So, watched by the cows, we carried several armfuls of hay from the barn and laid it out as a mattress under the ground sheet, then spread out the blankets and car rug. It began to look quite inviting. 'There you are!' said Gavin. 'It'll be great!'

Feeling pleased with ourselves, we returned to the restaurant where the Chief Fairy and Christine were dawdling over a second cup of coffee and watching the TV. This time Laurence Olivier was on, a very young Olivier, and also speaking immaculate French - another masterpiece of dubbing which was amusingly weird to watch. We grew quite hypnotised by the fluent and voluble stream of French tumbling from his lips, when we knew all the time - since we'd seen the film before - that everything he had said he had spoken in his flawless English.

The evening passed pleasantly. The plump, cheerful manageress proved chatty and accommodating, and much to the delight of the Chief Fairy spoke good English. At last she had another woman to talk to. Because her own French is non-existent she had been virtually struck dumb in company since our arrival in France - and there was even a move to make it the official language at home! But now at last she was able to chat away happily, and she made the most of the bonus.

At 10.30 I suggested we retire to our tent so that we could be up early and on our way to Spain the next morning. We said our goodnights and left the restaurant. It was almost pitch black, so I collected my car torch and set off into the field, the family following behind me in single file.

'Where's the tent?' said the Chief Fairy, after we'd been

picking our way carefully across the field for a couple of minutes.

'It should be round about here,' I said, peering around me and trying to make out a shape in the darkness. I couldn't make one out anywhere. 'This is damned silly,' I said. 'It was definitely round about here.'

'Oh, lord, don't say somebody's pinched it!' the Chief Fairy groaned. We stumbled around in the dark for a bit then suddenly there was a cry - part triumph and part anguish.

'Here it is!' shouted Gavin. 'Cor, look at it!'

I turned back. I'd passed it and the reason I'd passed it was simple enough. The tent was flat on the ground, with blankets and hay strewn all over the place. I flashed my torch on the chaos.

'What on earth . . . ?' began the Chief Fairy.

'Oh, God!' I groaned. I suddenly realised what had happened. It was those stupid cows. They'd nuzzled under the tent and pulled all the hay out. Not only had they eaten our mattress they'd kicked down all the guy ropes and the tent poles while they'd been stuffing themselves.

I looked up, flashing my torch around the field, but there wasn't a cow in sight. The villains had vanished. The only trace of them was the usual calling card which they'd left near the ground sheet. Unfortunately for him, Gavin was the first to discover this.

He stood in it in the dark and I heard a low moan of anguish. 'Isn't that just like a blasted French cow!' he said bitterly, surveying his foot by my torch light.

Normally, his mother or I would have told him off for swearing, but we hadn't the heart. His great tent idea lay in ruins and his foot ponged something shocking.

There was nothing for it but to start all over again. While Christine held the torch, Gavin and I hoisted the tent up and groped in the gloom for the tent pegs, keeping a wary eye for pancakes. At last we got it up to our satisfaction and returned to the barn to draw a new mattress.

There was no doubt the hay was a good idea because once

we'd spread it out again and the blankets were down on the ground sheet, it was very comfortable. We changed into our night things and settled down to sleep.

Once in the night I awoke stifled and realised we would all be in danger of suffocating in the small tent if we didn't get more ventilation, so I crawled over the slumbering bodies to pin back the tent flaps at the door. Outside it was still pitch black, but all was peace and quiet. I crawled back in and went to sleep.

I would like to say that I slept easily, but I didn't. I was tormented by a nightmare - the pressures of the day again, I suppose. I dreamed I had been captured and brought before a court of the Spanish Inquisition. They kept asking me how many pesetas made five and I said I couldn't tell them. They didn't believe me and put me through all sorts of tortures, the Rack, the Iron Maiden and finally, the Dreaded Bastinado, where they whip your feet. I awoke in a sweat and stared about me. It was dawn.

My mind took a few seconds to adjust to the strange surroundings, then I looked quickly at the open tent flaps and saw the reason for my nightmare - the Bastinado. It was one of those idiot cows tearing at the hay under my bare feet. They'd returned to breakfast on our new mattress.

I leapt from the blankets, and crawled quickly outside, shouting 'Gitoutofit!' If I'd had any sense or forethought I'd have done it more quietly. The cows jumped in terror and ran off mooing and tripping over the guy ropes again.

Slowly, but quite majestically, the whole tent collapsed on everybody and I was left standing on the grass outside in my pyjamas and bare feet.

At this point it began to rain.

12 We Spring a Leak

A plaintive voice cried out from under the folds of canvas. 'What's happened?' It was Christine.

'It's the cows,' I said. 'They've kicked over the guy ropes again.' I was trying to pin the tent pegs back and as I bent to the task I could feel large drops of rain falling on the back of my pyjamas. Almost at once the valley echoed to a distant boom of thunder. A heavy, black cloud was rolling up from the south-west. I knew somebody who wasn't going to like this - the Chief Fairy. She hates thunder. She creeps into dark corners at the slightest hint of one at home. Such is her infectious terror, she even has the cat scuttling into dark corners to cover its ears.

Inside the collapsed tent there was a muttering, grumbling, a bobbing of heads and feet and a sudden angry cry from Christine, 'Get off! You're kneeling on my arm!' then Gavin's face appeared under the tent walls. 'Were they eating the hay again?' he asked.

'Yes,' I said. 'Quick, lift that tent pole upright inside!' He crawled back in. 'Hurry!' I said. 'I'm getting wet out here!'

'I can't lift it up, let out some more slack on the guy rope!' he said, and I did so. Suddenly the tent began to rise again at one end.

'Now the other end! Quick!' I said, leaping across the wet grass to another guy rope. This end went up similarly and I crawled quickly back into the tent.

The Chief Fairy was now wide awake and looking at me big-eyed with terror. 'Was that thunder?'

'Yes,' I said, and as if to emphasise the point there was another louder boom overhead. She groaned and threw back her blankets. 'Oh, God, let's get out of here!'

'It's only six o'clock in the morning,' I said.

'I don't care, I'm not staying here in a thunderstorm,' she said decidedly.

Some of her panic began to infect the kids and they started dressing hurriedly, flinging aside blankets, diving for socks, shirts and trousers. With three of them at it in the confined space, thrashing about on their knees and half standing up, the tent was in grave danger of being uprooted again. 'Watch out!' I said, grabbing one of the tilting tent poles. 'You'll have it round our ears again!'

The rain was now drumming solidly on the canvas and at another crash of thunder the Chief Fairy flinched and moaned again.

'Look, you'll be all right here,' I said. 'We're low down in the valley and we're well clear of any trees if that's what's worrying you.'

'I am not staying here!'

'But you'll get drenched out there!' I protested. 'Listen to it! We might as well wait till it passes over. At least we'll be dry!'

At that moment there was a yelp of protest from Christine, who was struggling into her jeans. 'That's what *you* think! Look!' She held out her bare arm. Globules of water were running down it. We looked up. She was right. The tent was leaking. It had obviously been so long out of use that its waterproof properties, if any, had gone. Water was dripping from the roof seams and fine sprays spreading everywhere under the force of the deluge.

'Oh, God!' I groaned, defeated. We'd have to go. If we stayed packed in here it would be like a Turkish bath. Steam was already rising from my pyjamas.

I now relinquished my duty as tent-pole holder and joined the general scrum to get dressed. My entry into the confusion seemed to boost it with an additional urgency - caused perhaps not least by the fact that the man with his finger in the dyke had quit his post. Arms and legs flew about in the confined space as everybody scrambled into their clothes. Cries of 'Where's my other sock?' 'You're sitting on my pullover!' 'Stop poking me in the eye!' rang out from beneath the bumping canvas, while the Chief Fairy's eyes rolled at further crashes of thunder. Outside the rain fell in torrents.

By the time we were dressed the tent poles had been uprooted and we were supporting the canvas with our heads and shoulders. With more hopping about and hay flying everywhere, we rolled the blankets and pyjamas into the ground sheet. 'Here,' I said to the Chief Fairy, giving her the car keys. 'You and Christine dash to the car with these and Gavin and I will roll up the tent.'

'I'll get saturated doing that!' Gavin protested.

'What do you think's going to happen to me?' I said. 'Come on, it was your idea! "The tent will be great!" you said.'

'Oh, blimey!' he groaned.

So while his mother and sister fled across the field clutching our belongings, Gavin and I jumped about in the downpour pulling out the tent pegs. Then we too fled, leaving the cows to breakfast on the rest of our mattress.

I just hoped that we'd both get heroic mentions in that holiday essay.

Alas, our troubles did not end with our flight from the camping site. Our first urgent need was to find somewhere to change into dry clothes and, hopefully, to get some breakfast. But it was 6.30 in the morning and our cosy restaurant of the night before was shut. There was nothing for it but to press on through the rain until we found somewhere open.

Two hours later, still heading for Spain, we found ourselves in Toulouse. In a traffic jam. In the rush hour. In the rain. Such a traffic jam had to be seen to be believed. Travelling for the past week along the clear, open country roads, with long, straight stretches, we had often wondered where all the French cars were. In Toulouse we found out. They were all here.

Never have I seen traffic like it. With no by-pass, everything - but everything - goes through Toulouse. Lane after lane of cars, lorries and buses were jammed solid in street after street, all of it moving forward at what seemed like three yards every five minutes.

Damp, untidy and hungry as we were, this is all we needed to complete our misery, and tempers began to explode. Sitting in that traffic jam was like being boiled in an emotional pressure cooker. Everybody was snarling at everybody, but most of all everybody was snarling at me.

Somehow they all traced it back to my £20 wine splurge. If I hadn't been so blind and stupid, if I'd read the menu properly, I wouldn't have been forever counting my money on café tables to see what we could afford and what we couldn't afford. People wouldn't have been denied the comfort of a proper bed and food and a roof over their heads instead of a sopping wet collapsing tent and no breakfast.

Whatever the cost, everybody snapped and snarled, tonight we would invest in warm, dry B and B at a proper hotel. All inspirations about tents in fields with mattress-chewing cows would be ignored. Definitely. In the meantime the quicker everybody got into some dry clothes and sat down to a hot breakfast the quicker everybody would be pleased, everybody said, looking at me.

To keep the rebellion at bay, I decided I'd better make sure we had the money for all this luxury and pulled briefly out of the steaming traffic jam to change some pesetas into francs at a bank. My four days supply of pesetas had now dwindled down to one and I fervently hoped we'd be able to cash a cheque once we reached Spain.

An hour later we drew up - and a pretty bedraggled crew we were - outside a roadhouse to the south of Toulouse. Unwashed, half-combed, hayseed still clinging to our damp and crumpled clothes, we looked and felt like a bunch of half-drowned gipsies. And bad-tempered ones, too. So much for the tent life.

Happily, once inside, our daily question, '*Où se trouve la toilette, s'il vous plaît?*' revealed spacious, modern washrooms where we were able to wash and change into fresh, dry clothes. Oddly, our unkempt condition and procession to the separate washrooms, loaded with clean clothes from the car, created little stir - no doubt they're used to the English arriving like this.

Soon, in a better frame of mind, we were sitting down to an excellent breakfast of ham omelettes and coffee.

Over breakfast I studied the map. We had now travelled some 900 miles since leaving London. Another 160 miles, about four hours driving, would take us to the Spanish border. Once into Spain, what I had in mind was to head for a little village on the Costa Brava, of which friends of ours had spoken highly. Indeed, they had built their own little villa there, where they were spend-Easter with their two children. Before we had all set off they had said: 'If you should reach that far down do call in to see us.' I had never been sure that we *would* reach that far in the light of the various upsets we'd faced, but now that we were within striking distance the idea was appealing to me - indeed, it was appealing to all of us. Perhaps we might even stay there a couple of days. There would be new company for everybody - which might at least take the heat off me.

As we discussed the idea over our omelettes the mood of anticipation grew stronger. The mere word 'Spain' had a magic ring for Gavin. Though the rest of us had been there before, he had not, as he had so vociferously pointed out at the start of the tour. He had heard about it only from friends in school who wrote their holiday essays about such places. But he knew it was a land of sun and sand, of oranges and dark-skinned peasants and, most of all, the warm waters of the Mediterranean. For this pleasure particularly he had brought along his swimming goggles, schnorkel breathing tube and flippers.

Certainly, omens for the sun looked good. An English couple, seated at an adjacent table, overheard our conversation and joined in to say that they had just been touring Spain and when they'd left it the day before the weather had been glorious. They had sun tans to prove it, too. They then offered the children oranges from a large bag of them which they had bought in the market at dirt-cheap prices.

'Ooh, thanks!' said Gavin, who is partial to an orange.

'You'll be able to buy those yourself in the market tomorrow morning,' the man said. 'About two a penny.'

'Great!' said Gavin.

We thanked the couple for their kindness and returned to the car. The rain had stopped. With a bit of luck we should reach our friends comfortably by late afternoon. 'And won't they be surprised to see us?' said Christine. 'I'll bet they never thought we'd get this far.'

'Neither did I?' I said.

Soon we were speeding across the broad, fast road that links Toulouse with the ancient city of Carcassonne, passing vineyard after vineyard spread out in the gently undulating countryside. We were following a parallel course to the Canal du Midi, built in the 17th century to connect the Atlantic to the Mediterranean.

On we went through Carcassonne, by-passing the port of Narbonne and across the wind-swept coastal plain to Perpignan, the last French town before the Spanish border. Here, beneath the snow-capped Pyrenees, which we had watched growing closer and closer, we stopped for a lunch-time snack.

Perpignan is an attractive town with broad avenues and palms dotted ornamentally about them. After our snack at a pavement café we strolled in the warm sunshine that had at last broken through the clouds. We also took the opportunity to send a few postcards home . . . 'Having wonderful time . . . ' It's wonderful what the holidaymaker can overlook!

As we were about to return to our parked car, Gavin ran excitedly from a souvenir shop. 'Dad! Can I have my pocket money back? You've got francs now, haven't you?'

I fished in my pocket for his 5 francs 40 centimes, which he had lent me after the wine-night calamity. 'What do you want it for?' I asked.

'There's a marvellous sombrero in that window. Come and see! It looks great!'

We followed him back to the shop window. It was a handsome piece of headgear all right, bright green, gaily trimmed with yellow and a turned up brim as wide as his shoulders. 'You can't afford that,' I said, looking at the price tag, 'it's 36 francs!'

'I know,' he said quickly, 'but if you lend me 30 francs and 60 centimes I can pay you back from my Post Office savings book when we get home, can't I?'

He saw us all looking doubtful. 'That's a lot of money for something you'll probably only wear once or twice,' said the Chief Fairy, who is well experienced in his crazes.

'No, I won't! I'll wear it all the time!' he protested. 'It'll keep me from getting sunstroke, won't it?'

It seemed an unlikely danger. However, I said, 'All right, it's your money,' and followed him into the shop. He picked up an identical hat inside and tried it on, looking at his reflection in a showcase mirror. A big smile spread across his face. '*Ah, senor! Muchas gracias! Si si! Una momento!*' he said in fractured Spanish, then spun round laughing.

'Where did you pick that up?' I said.

'I've heard it in school,' he said. 'Some of the boys know lots of Spanish.'

Ah, yes, those hot essay kids.

'All right, there you are,' I said, handing him the money.

He paid for his green sombrero and said he didn't want it wrapped up, he'd just keep it on his head.

'*Merci!*' said the assistant.

'Mercy buckets!' Gavin replied cheerfully and marched out of the shop. 'And *muchas gracias!*' He was feeling pretty cock-a-hoop about his mastery of French and all set now to make an assault on Spanish.

I estimated it would take us less than an hour to reach the Spanish frontier, but I estimated without our atrocious luck. There must have been something pretty hideous in our stars that day, which had started with our early morning tent disaster - because now we ran out of road!

We were half-way to the border town of La Junquera, which nestles in the foothills between the Mediterranean and the Pyrenees, and I was trying to draw everybody's attention to a particularly attractive view of the snow-capped mountains.

'Where?' said Christine.

'Watch the road,' said the Chief Fairy.

'Over there,' I said, nodding out of the window.

'I can't see them - where?' said Christine, craning to look.

'There! Are you blind?' and I jerked round in my seat to point out of the rear window.

'The corner! Watch the corner!' the Chief Fairy screamed in my ear. 'You're too close!' But it was too late. A sharp bend had loomed up from nowhere and I was suddenly bumping on the hard shoulder of the road which gave way to a gravel embankment that sloped steeply down to a ditch. I braked hard, the car skidded and jerked to a halt, but tilting dangerously over the ditch.

'Everybody out!' I shouted. 'No, this side, this side!'

They clambered out in a panic and I jammed the car in gear before getting out to inspect our plight.

'God, I told you to watch the road!' said the Chief Fairy.

'All right, all right, don't panic, we're all safe,' I said.

'How are you going to drive it out of there?' she said, voicing a question that was in my mind too. The children looked on anxiously.

'I don't know,' I said, 'but I can try. You stay up here.' I skidded down on the gravel and climbed gingerly behind the wheel.

'Be careful!' she called out.

I revved the engine and let the clutch out, but the wheels began to spin on the sloping gravel and Christine shrieked, 'It's slipping down the hill, daddy! Get out!'

I jammed the brake on again and climbed back up the embankment. 'We're going to need a tow out of that,' I said.

We all looked at each other, then Gavin exploded, 'That's you and your boring scenery for you! If you'd kept your eyes on the road like mum said instead of looking at stupid mountains we wouldn't have crashed!'

'All right, all right,' I said. 'Keep your shirt on!'

He swung round on Christine, 'And if you hadn't been so blind you'd have seen the stupid things instead of asking him - where, where, where?' he said with bitter mimicry.

'Oh, shut up!' she said.

'Heavens, what a mess!' moaned their mother. 'We were lucky we weren't killed.'

Tempers were now even more prickly than they had been in our Toulouse traffic jam.

'Calm down, everybody,' I said, 'I'll see if we can get some help.' I waved to several cars but they sped by. 'You might as well sit down, this could take a bit of time,' I told my glum-faced crew.

I continued trying to flag for some help, and once a Mercedes, travelling in the opposite direction, slowed down and called something out of the window, but his French was too rapid for me to follow. I was thinking of setting off back to the nearest village when a van answered my wave and pulled up.

The driver was a young, efficient-looking fellow and quickly sized up the problem, with the aid of some of my fractured French. He backed up his van to the embankment edge, then pulled out a rope and quickly secured it to the front of my car. He signalled me to get behind the wheel. I did so - once again gingerly - but this time there was no slithering back. The rope taughtened as the van moved forward and the car came back on the road with ease. I breathed a sigh of relief. It had been much easier than I had anticipated. I thanked him profusely and offered to pay for his assistance, but he declined with a smile. He was happy to be of service, he said. As he climbed back into his van he added something about reporting to the police, waved goodbye and drove off.

'Did you catch that, Christine?' I said. 'What he said just then?'

'He said you should report the accident to the police.'

I vaguely recalled something about having to report even the slightest mishap to the police if you were in France, but I shrugged, I couldn't see the point. We were almost out of France anyway.

'Never mind, let's forget it,' I said. 'There's no damage. We might as well press on. We've only a few miles to do.'

I would have been less cavalier about French traffic laws had I been able to see the scene a few miles behind me. That Mercedes driver who had called to me as he passed had apparently reported our plight on his way through the next town and a police car was now speeding up behind us. We heard its siren screaming as we approached the border, though thinking it had nothing to do with us - until it began to flag us down!

'Oh, dear!' said the Chief Fairy. 'You should have reported the accident! Now you've done it!'

'We'll probably all finish up in jail!' said Gavin, folding his arms and now utterly defeatist.

'Be quiet!' I said. 'How could I report the accident? It only happened ten minutes ago and I haven't seen anybody to report it to!'

I pulled in to the roadside as the police car swerved up and halted ahead of us. A gendarme approached. Gavin groaned again, Christine nibbled her nails and deep anxiety creased the Chief Fairy's brow. If she could have waved a wand now to get us out of it she would have done.

But, at last, something cheerful. The gendarme said he'd heard of our mishap running off the road and was everybody all right? They had been concerned about us. Oh, yes, we said, with great sighs of relief, we were all right. He smiled and said that was good then, they didn't want anything to happen to their tourists. He wished us all a happy holiday and waved us on.

'Now everybody relax. You all worry over nothing,' I said.

It took us only a few minutes now to reach La Junquera on the Spanish frontier and we drove slowly through it fascinated. It looks like a Wild West border town. The first thing that strikes you is the evidence of its main trade - changing money. Every few yards down the main street, billboards, signs and flashing lights beckon the traveller - in several languages - to change his money at the innumerable little offices and street counters. It's a bit like a mini Las Vegas.

Since the only currency I had left was pesetas, and precious few of those now, we had no reason to stop, but a little farther on we had to pull up at the Customs checkpoint.

I always feel a sense of undiscovered villainy whenever I'm questioned by Customs men, even though I may be totally innocent. The moment an official approaches me or bends to address me in my car I feel goosepimples rising on my neck. 'Anything to declare, sir?' and the prickling sensation grows stronger, as it did in this case, though I may still have been suffering from our recent scare with the gendarmes.

'No,' I said.

'Nothing?'

His eyes, which had seemed to be searching my very soul - they always seem to be searching my very soul - flicked round the car and the passengers. I felt my mouth go dry. I had a sudden fear that he would want to examine the car and discover something I had either forgotten or didn't know about.

'No perfume, jewellery? Nothing you've bought in France that you're bringing into Spain?'

The more they question, the guiltier I feel, and now I come to think of it I suppose it must have more to do with the embarrassment of having your honesty put on the rack - like a schoolmaster quizzing a small boy - rather than a criminal versus the law relationship. It's the creepy business of being exposed as a liar and a cad in front of everybody.

Once during the war I stood behind an Army captain in the Customs shed at Southampton after we had all disembarked from the *Île de France*. 'Anything to declare, sir?' said the Customs man. 'No,' the officer said firmly - perhaps too firmly. Between them, on the table, lay the captain's suitcases like an undisclosed hand of poker dice. The captain had called his hand and assumed, no doubt, that the Customs man was gentleman enough to accept it.

Alas for the captain, he didn't. 'Would you mind opening this one, sir?' he said. I saw the captain's face go red as he fumbled with the keys. The Customs man opened the case and there beneath a silk dressing gown were eight bottles of whisky. He looked up, very slowly, at the captain. I cringed in embarrassment for him. 'Would you mind coming this way, sir?' he said politely.

It was all too much for me. When I moved up to the Customs officer I couldn't blurt out quick enough, 'I've got six pairs of nylons and a bottle of perfume!' And I opened the suitcase to show him. I'll never make a smuggler.

'No, nothing,' I said to the Spanish official now. 'Not a thing.'

'Yes, there is!' Gavin said loudly in the back seat and my heart nearly stopped.

The Customs man leaned in. '*Si?*'

'There's this sombrero and a packet of crisps,' said Gavin urgently. He was ever a stickler for the truth. The Customs man smiled and said there would be no charge, but as I pulled away from the checkpoint my goosepimples were going full prickle.

'Lord, I wondered what on earth he was going to say then,' the Chief Fairy muttered. 'I went quite cold.'

'You should feel *me!*' I said.

'Well, you're supposed to declare things, aren't you?' said Gavin. I think our recent encounter with the law was still in his mind.

'If it's necessary,' I said. 'You leave the declaring to me!'

'And suppose you forget and we all finish up in a Spanish jail!' he retorted.

'At least,' I said, feeling a bit easier now, 'it'll be drier than a tent.'

'Anything would be better than that!' Christine declared feelingly.

* * *

At last, following our friends' route directions down the Costa Brava coastline, we came upon their little village and the white-painted villa they had built overlooking the sea. It was late afternoon and my friend John, his wife Amanda and their two children were having tea on their patio as we drove up. With them was a friend, a tall, distinguished fellow, who turned out to be a local Spanish businessman named Carlos.

Our friends were delighted and surprised to see us. John rose from his sunbed, grinning and removing his sunglasses. 'Well, well, you made it! *Buenos dias, amigos!*'

'You're just in time for tea!' smiled Amanda. We sighed and said thank you - except Gavin. He raised his green sombrero and said, '*Muchas gracias, Senora!*'

'Why, that's very good, Gavin - very good!' said Amanda. 'Isn't it Carlos?' She turned to the tall Spaniard who had risen from his chair at our arrival. He smiled and said: 'Excellent - a perfect accent!'

While Gavin blushed, Amanda introduced Carlos to us. We shook hands, then he turned to the Chief Fairy and with impeccable ease took her hand, bowed over it gently and kissed it. 'Enchanted, senora! *Bella, mucha bella!*' he murmured in a riveting accent.

I didn't actually see them but I'll swear the Chief Fairy's goosepimples came up like button mushrooms.

'Oh,' she said weakly, making no attempt to withdraw her hand, 'I think I'm going to like it here!'

Eyeing the suave Spaniard and the dreamy look in my wife's eyes, I wasn't quite sure myself.

13 Waiter! Kiss My Hand!

There was no doubt my friends John and Amanda had not oversold this little village. It was a delight, a picture postcard paradise tucked off the tourist route and totally unspoiled. In the centre was a marvellous, tiny Spanish square, cobble-stoned and tree-shaded where you could sit and drink at the tables served by the three inns which bordered the square. On the fourth side was an old Spanish church, which looked out over a sandy beach towards Africa.

Three miles away was a fishing port, which also offered the customary tourist attractions of restaurants and nightlife.

With our friends' aid, we established ourselves in a holiday apartment on the ground floor of an old farmhouse. It nestled in a wooded setting half a mile from the village square and beach, and was to be our home for the next five days. Indeed, it was also to be our home for another fortnight, later in the summer, when we returned - so enchanted were we with our stay. There was everything here for the family holidaymaker - the sun and sand, safe, warm bathing, a village peace and excellent Spanish food at the three inns. And, as we were to discover, very cheap, too.

Once in the farmhouse, our first big relief was to be able to unpack everything and stow it in wardrobes and drawers. For the past week we'd been living out of suitcases - all of them.

Here I'd made something of a planning error. Because each one of the family had a suitcase - sometimes two - packed with their own things, even down to toothbrushes, we had had to carry them all into every hotel where we had made an overnight stop. When this laden procession staggered through the door it looked as though we were arriving for the summer, and many a Gallic eyebrow was raised at the reception desk when we said, no, we'd just come for the night.

'One night, *m'sieu?*' queried a reception clerk in Brittany.

'We always travel like this,' I assured him. I nearly added 'on picnics, too', then thought better of it. But obviously it would make more sense on our journey to put all our overnight things in one suitcase and leave the rest in the car boot, as I've no doubt sensible motoring tourists do all the time. But we were new to the game.

We were now looking forward to spending the next few days in one place. That first night we arranged to dine with our friends and their children in one of the village inns. Much to the Chief Fairy's delight, the magnetic, hand-kissing Carlos, who lived in a fine house locally, came along too. He arrived while we were having an aperitif in the bar.

'*Buenas noches,*' he smiled, kissing the ladies' hands and turning the Chief Fairy's knees to water again.

'What a beautiful language,' she sighed. 'It sounds so much nicer than "good evening"!'

'Not when you say "good evening", senora,' he murmured, and I thought this fellow will have to go!

'Come on,' said John, 'let's get stuck into the nosh.' So we all moved into the restaurant.

The village inn was as charming inside as it was outside. It was full of those lovely Spanish arches, alcoves, wrought-iron room dividers and cool, mosaic floors. There were nine of us for dinner and we were served by two young Spanish waiters, dark-haired, white-coated and impeccably fresh and clean. Despite this five-star service and attention, the bill was ridiculously cheap. A variety of Spanish dishes were offered on the menu, which Carlos was happy to explain to us. We listened impressed at his knowledge - to say nothing of his charm - then finally settled for starters of succulent local white fish and the house paella (which Gavin at last got to taste for his essay).

This all went down splendidly with a carafe of the local white wine - also laughably cheap at about 20p. It brought to mind my last encounter with white wine at dinner and I recounted the tale of the mis-read wine list. My friends laughed. I felt obliged to point out that it wasn't so funny at the time. At which my friends laughed even louder. 'Oh, I think that's really very amusing!' said Carlos.

Truly, everything is funny provided it happens to somebody else.

'We've been paying for it ever since!' complained Gavin, who really wasn't amused at all. 'Whenever I want something mum says, "No, you can't have that, we're still paying for your father's bottles of wine"!'

'You still haven't paid me back my pocket money either,' Christine reminded me. 'You borrowed that to pay the bill!'

'To say nothing,' the Chief Fairy added for good measure, 'of having to sleep in a field because we had no more francs left. *And* in a thunderstorm. I've never been so scared in all my life! I thought we were all going to be struck dead!'

Carlos seemed to be enjoying himself hugely. 'I expect you'll be a little more careful ordering your wine in future!' he laughed.

'That's why I'm letting you do it,' I said.

There was more laughter - in fact, we did a lot of laughing that night. I didn't mind the jokes about my wine disaster because I now felt considerable relief. John had said we could solve my financial crisis at a bank in the neighbouring fishing port next day. They would cash a cheque for me.

'I must say,' said the Chief Fairy, 'I've never known him count his money so much! It was never out of his hand!'

'And the way you lot were eating, it didn't stay there very long,' I was moved to retort. 'No wonder I was counting!'

'Now, now!' said John, stepping in as referee. 'This is a nice peaceful village, don't ruin it!'

After dinner Carlos suggested we move outside for liqueurs. The night was warm and still, and we sat under the stars at the *al fresco* tables in the square. Here, despite John's claim that it was a peaceful village, we learned of an intriguing war going on among the three pubs.

The wicker chairs provided at the tables for customers were blue, brown and white. Each inn had its own colour and if you sat in a brown chair you didn't get served by a blue chair waiter, though all the chairs were jumbled together under the trees in the same pint-sized square. It didn't affect us so much now because we were visiting out of the peak season and the service was excellent, but in August when the little square was bustling with visitors, it could make quite a difference which coloured chair you sat in. If you found you were having to wait too long for the champagne cocktails to come up, you moved to a colour where the service was faster.

However, on the advice of my friend John, a most diplomatic fellow, we tried to spread our custom equally among the rival chairs so as not to show favouritism. In village life it's quite important.

In the summer months there were other hazards, too. Well, with the main street running through the centre of three bars, I suppose there would be. Few cars came through - there just wasn't room - but when they did they were always liable to mow down a tray of gin and tonics; to say nothing of the waiter hurrying across the square with them. The drinks are cheap enough, of course, but the waiters come a bit more expensive!

I was nearly a victim myself one night. We were sipping drinks with John and his family when a German tourist, driving across the cobbled square, nudged my chair and I was thrust against the table. I turned - more irritated than shaken - to remonstrate with the fellow, but he had moved on.

One of the blue-chair waiters hurried to the table. 'Are you all right, *senor*?' I assured him I was and adjusted my seat again.

'To think,' mused John, 'you survive a war and German bullets and German guns and they run you down in a bar!'

The waiter said, 'Ah, some of these Germans - no manners, *senor*. I am sorry.'

'Don't worry about it,' I said. 'At least I was going down fighting in true-blue British tradition.' I held up my brandy glass, still clutched unspilt in my hand.

He bowed courteously, moving back to join the other waiters

on the fringes of the tables. With some pleasure I had already observed the manner and dress of these Spanish waiters. They looked extremely smart in their freshly-laundered shirts, white jackets, bow ties and black hair neatly combed. They were cheerful, attentive and all young. This one, I thought, couldn't have been more than 17.

'What a charming fellow,' I said and hoped that my children had noticed his solicitousness for me. This was the sort of example of younger generation concern which I had hoped to expose my family to when we first set out across the Continent. I hadn't found it in France, but here it was in Spain. Clearly, they brought their children up well here. This one wouldn't sit on his father's death bed playing cards, or criticise the wine he bought, or jeer at his handling of fresh crab. Not this one.

'Yes, he's very nice, I agree,' said the Chief Fairy. 'They're all charming, but you don't suppose all that attention was just for you, do you?'

'What do you mean?' I said. The others laughed - except Christine, who quietly blushed. Obviously things had been going on which I had failed to see.

'He hasn't been able to take his eyes off her since we sat down,' smiled Amanda, then turned good-naturedly to Christine. 'Isn't that right, Christine?'

'Oh, nonsense!' she said and blushed again.

'The Spanish love blondes,' said John with a wink, 'you should do all right here, Christine!'

'Don't be ridiculous!' she retorted. But I quickly realised it wasn't ridiculous at all. For the rest of the holiday we had marvellous service at the blue chairs. Whenever we sat down the young Spanish waiter was there at once, no matter who else was tapping the table for service. Well, I suppose if you have a daughter you're entitled to the odd bonus or two.

For her part, Christine suddenly developed a keen interest in sitting down on blue wicker chairs and drinking minerals at all times of the day and night. She kept running out of pesetas to buy herself Cokes and would come to me urgently to replenish her purse. Each day she grew browner and blonder and more radiant from sitting in the sun in the square, and receiving royal service from that young dark-eyed waiter, whose name we learned was Manuel.

What they talked about I've no idea, but she did a lot of writing in her diary. Whenever we stretched out to sunbathe on the beach, or on the grass in front of our farmhouse for a siesta, the diary came out. What went in remained a secret though it was Gavin's opinion it would be a lot of tosh.

'He calls me Christina,' she sighed one day after lunch. 'That's Spanish for Christine, isn't it?'

I said I suppose it was. 'Christina . . . Christina . . . ' she murmured, then rose and said she felt like a Coke and would go into the village and have one.

'Surprise, surprise!' muttered Gavin, who was busy writing up his essay notes.

After our siesta we wandered down to the village to pick up Christine for a swim. The square was almost empty - most sensible people were still enjoying their siesta - but Christine and Manuel were sitting talking at a table together. She rose and said goodbye with a shy smile. He took her hand, bowed over it and gallantly kissed it. 'Cor!' said Gavin, as his sister came towards us as though floating on a cloud. 'They're all at it - waiters as well! What a soppy way to go on!'

'Oh, I don't know,' murmured the Chief Fairy, 'I think it's rather nice - very nice!' She dreamily touched the back of her own hand. Her eyes had that 'tilt' sign again - but Carlos was nowhere in sight.

14 Pardon My Franish Panic!

Next day we drove to the neighbouring fishing port cum tourist resort to cash a cheque, draw pesetas, do some shopping - and weigh the Chief Fairy. That is, if we could find some scales.

She was anxious to see what damage had been done by all the tasty dishes she'd so wantonly eaten. She wasn't fooling herself. She knew she was going to have to grit her teeth a bit when she stood on that weighing machine because she'd already had to move into her No. 2 holiday dresses - the ones for the return journey.

It was a bright, sunny morning with a soft breeze coming off the Mediterranean as we drove from the village along the narrow coast road - more of a dirt track actually since it was a secondary approach to the town. It was fringed by woods on one side and bright, burning sands on the other, and eventually brought us to the port's main street.

You could see at once that it was an old town, a town that had known poverty and violence. Much of it had been unchanged for decades. On the white, dusty walls of old Moorish architecture, where the sun glared back, you could still see bullet scars from the revolution of the thirties. It was a town of dark-complexioned faces, black shawls and heavy boots, and dogs ran about in the streets. But this was the unchanging heart of the town; the facade for tourists was on the front. There you found the smart bars and restaurants, pavement cafes and souvenir shops;

and overlooking the harbour, the inevitable high-rise holiday apartment blocks and hotels.

To reach the front we had to negotiate our way across a small square, a junction serving five roads, and it was here that Gavin saw his first Spanish policeman, directing traffic.

'Hey!' he laughed. 'Look at that hat!'

Since Gavin was wearing his green sombrero at the time I hardly felt that he had the right to criticise. However, I was prepared to concede that it was a funny looking hat all right. I've never been able to understand why Spanish policemen wear those things, flattened at the front (or is it the back? I can never remember) as though they've walked (or backed) into a brick wall. But I'm sure there's a rational explanation for them somewhere. I've just never inquired into it. Whenever I see them I always think of Buster Keaton as a torreador.

There was little traffic about and the policeman quickly waved us on, with Gavin grinning out of the window at him. The lad seemed to enjoy watching policemen on traffic duty; I recalled that he'd had a good chuckle at the agitated movements of 'Charlie Chaplin' in Cherbourg. But if he was amused by these it was nothing to the entertaining antics of a fellow we were to see on point duty in this same square later in the summer. Oh, a real star turn!

He was a small, dapper, dark-skinned fellow in a white jacket two sizes too big for him, an outsize white pith helmet held up by his ears and with a heavy revolver strapped to his side. A large black belt pulled tight round his middle completed an effect that suggested he wasn't so much wearing his clothes as tied up in them and trying to fight his way out.

Gavin and I spotted him as we strolled into the square - we were waiting for the Chief Fairy and Christine to come out of a shop.

'Oh, look at that helmet!' exclaimed Gavin. And truly it was enormous. If it hadn't been for the support of his ears the helmet would have been resting on his shoulders and the poor fellow wouldn't have seen any traffic at all. One felt like calling out jovially, 'Come out, I can see your feet!' But, of course, one didn't. In Spain you never know what they might run you in for.

But much more joy was to come. Despite his incongruous appearance, he obviously fancied himself as a point-duty man and was spinning elegantly round on his feet in the centre of the small square as traffic came at him from all directions. One moment he was a ballet dancer, summoning the traffic with airy flicks of his fingers and hands, pirouetting on one foot and blowing imperious blasts on the whistle stuck in his mouth - at least, I assumed it was his mouth; the blasts were issuing from beneath the brim of his pith helmet. The next moment he was a bull-fighter on his tiptoes, body arched, flourishing cars past him - 'Hey! Toro! Toro!' - and holding his ground to see how close each one could skim past his feet - 'Ole!' - without crunching them into the square. He had great style, this diminutive, dark-skinned cop.

We watched, vastly entertained for about 10 minutes, then it became apparent that something was going wrong with his act. Was it the pressure of the increasing traffic flow through the square? Instead of the elegant flourishes and pirouetting his movements became jerkier and more agitated, and he started to gesticulate furiously not only at the traffic but at the pedestrians trying to dodge through it.

He was growing angrier and browner under his outsize pith helmet, and between whistle blasts kept glancing towards the doors of an official-looking building on one side of the square. Was he, I wondered, whistling for his relief who perhaps was late on duty? At this point I didn't know, but his antics were now more those of a demented windmill rather than a torreador or ballet dancer. As a result the converging traffic began to get snarled up. They couldn't follow his flourishes.

Suddenly he stopped waving his arms and blowing his whistle and marched off the square. He walked straight up the steps of the official-looking building, leaving total chaos behind him. The traffic was locked solid and you may imagine the honking and the hooting that went on.

I waited for his relief to emerge. When he didn't I strolled - out of sheer idle curiosity - to the portals of the building and glanced inside. Gavin was similarly intrigued. After a minute or two our traffic torreador friend re-emerged, his agitation obviously subsided, and proceeded with his old style to unsnarl the traffic jam.

Whether another officer was supposed to relieve him or not, I don't know, but at least Gavin and I now knew the cause of his agitation. As we glanced inside the doors of the official building, we saw him emerging from an inside door, adjusting his dress, as they say, and doing a little jig on one leg. He'd got his relief all right.

Gavin giggled then said, 'If he'd been a French policeman he could have just stayed out in the square and done it, couldn't he? And gone on directing traffic with one hand!'

Our first essential task now was to lay our hands on more pesetas so we parked the car and set off in search of the bank that John had told me about. It lay up one of the narrow, cobbled streets off the sea-front, but our progress to it was slow. It was not only slow, it was expensive. The family kept stopping to examine the goods in the boutiques and souvenir shops and the dress shops and cake shops - well, you know how it is trying to get women past *any* kind of shop. The kids spotted souvenirs and knick-knacks they wanted to buy as presents for friends at home.

'Could I have my pocket money back now, please?' said Christine. 'In pesetas.'

'That reminds me,' said Gavin, examining his own small change, 'you didn't pay me last week's pocket money!'

'You've got it in your hand,' I said. He never stops trying.

'That's the week before!' he protested hotly. 'I want this week's! We've been travelling a week, you know, it's due again!'

Once more I thought, if only we had him as Chancellor, we'd never get into the mess we do get into - the country, I mean. So I forked out for both of them, and changed his francs, too.

'What rate of exchange are you giving me?' he asked suspiciously as I counted the grubby notes into his hand.

'The official rate,' I said. 'There you are, it's on that board over there - 171.70 to the pound.' He looked across the narrow street at the board outside a *Bureau de Change*, which listed the day's rate for all the currencies.

'Okay,' he said, after scrutinising it for a moment and satisfying himself that I wasn't chiselling him.

'I'll have mine back, too, if you don't mind,' said the Chief Fairy. 'And I'll need some more for shopping. Don't look so pained!'

By the time I'd redistributed the currency I was almost cleaned out. I just hoped that bank was going to come to the rescue.

Having been stripped of my peseta roll, I was now called upon to go into the shops and help the whole flush brood to spend it - in the role of interpreter. I had a feeling it wasn't going to be my day. My Spanish is, if anything, considerably worse than my French and what emerged was a sort of hybrid Franish, or maybe it was Spench. Anyway, it didn't get me very far - well, not at first.

A fancy cake in a pastry shop had caught the eye of the Chief Fairy - 'We could have that for tea this afternoon at the farmhouse,' she said - so I led the way into the shop.

A young, dark-eyed Spanish girl approached me, '*Senor?*'

'*Quanta questa,*' I began (I knew that was Spanish for 'how much?' but then I couldn't think of the words for 'is that chocolate cake in the window?' so I switched to French) '*ce gâteau chocolat dans la fenêtre* - (then, remembering the Spanish for 'please') - *por favor?*'

She looked at me blankly in much the same way as that cabbage-sweeping Frenchman had done in Cherbourg, then turned to speak to an older woman, rather smartly dressed - and I would guess the manageress - who was serving another customer.

'*Si, senor?*' said the older woman. I repeated my request while my family looked on. But this time I pointed to the cake in the window.

'Ah, that one, yes! It's 15 pesetas, sir!' she said in faultless English. Well, at least she'd understood! I turned to enjoy a moment of triumph in front of the family, but they seemed totally unimpressed. 'If I were you,' Christine muttered, 'I'd just stick to English, I'm sure most of them understand it.'

We bought the cake, a few souvenirs and, in a little market

square we came across, some of the splendid oranges we'd tasted the day before. They were ridiculously cheap, and this time bought with ease. All I did was point to them and say, '*Quanta questa?*'

The market woman, an old, black-shawled figure with a face wrinkled by age and sun, wrote the price down on a handy jotting pad. '*Diez pesetas, senor,*' she said, pointing to the figure '10' on her pad. I was pleased to note that this practice of writing down, as well as announcing it, was a popular one among traders and shopkeepers. They'd obviously had trouble before with tourists like me. At least the written figure is international.

Even so, I still found myself scrutinising their pads very closely to make sure I'd got the price right. The memory of those £10 bottles of wine was still with me.

It was just after we'd made these purchases that the Chief Fairy suddenly said: 'Oh, there's one look!'

'There's one what?' I said.

'A weighing machine!'

'Oh, lord,' groaned Gavin, 'not that again! Diets, diets, diets! That's all you ever talk about! Can't you think of anything else?'

I must confess the boy had a point. He certainly gets his fill at home. From the first roll of tumblers on the bathroom scales in the morning - and the faint gasp 'Oh, lord, I'm up another pound!' - to the groans that accompany the food commercials on TV at night, the subject is never far away. One morning at breakfast he dropped his knife and fork in exasperation and said, 'How can I enjoy this food when you're going on about its stupid calories all the time!'

Now, having made his protest, he marched off up the street to look in another souvenir shop, while his mother prepared to do battle with the weighing machine. And I mean battle. First she handed me her shopping bag, then her handbag, then her summer cardigan, then her bracelet (she *never* takes on a weighing machine without stripping for action). Finally, she stepped onto the platform and watched the needle whiz round.

There was a sharp intake of breath. 'Good heavens, what's that?' she exclaimed, staring at the figures. 'Fifty-four!' For one horrible moment she thought it was fifty-four stones!

'That's kilos,' I said, 'You'll have to convert it to pounds.'

'What's that then?' she frowned.

'Well, let's see there are . . . ' - I turned to Christine - 'how many pounds in a kilo, just over two, isn't it?'

'Two-point-three pounds per kilo,' said Christine.

'So what's that in stones and pounds?' the Chief Fairy asked, still frowning.

'Er - two-point-three - er - times 54 - is - is - hang on let me scribble it down. Anybody got a pencil?' I gave her a pen. 'And a bit of paper?' I fished in my pocket for an envelope.

The three of us stood at the weighing machine while this sum was worked out. 'Nine stones!' said Christine triumphantly. Ah, the boons of an expensive education!

'Nine stones!' gasped the Chief Fairy. 'Oh, that's terrible! There must be something wrong with the machine! Here, you try it,' she said, turning to me.

It's an old trick this, using me as a calibrator when she suspects the machine of dishonesty, but we'd wasted enough time already. If we didn't get a move on, the bank would be shutting up shop for its siesta. 'Of course there's nothing wrong with the machine!' I said. 'Come on!'

Reluctantly, she stepped from the platform muttering, 'I can't have put on six pounds in a week, I'm sure that figure's wrong.' I resisted the temptation to say if that figure was lying, hers was not - wasn't she in her No. 2 dresses already? - but you've got to be a bit careful what you say at sensitive moments like this. Not that I'm complaining; I like 'em plumpish. Not too much, mind you, but enough. Something that shows the curves anyway, not the beanpole style. That maybe all right for the fashion plates, but not for practical living.

'You're all right, forget about it, the shape's fine,' I said, by way of comfort. 'You're on holiday, enjoy yourself.'

* * *

We moved on and came at last to the bank. It looked rather busy inside, so I said, 'You wait here, I'll be out in a jiffy.' Some jiffy! Whatever traumatic shock the Chief Fairy had sustained over allegedly false figures paled beside the one I had over the bank's figures. Oh, they changed my cheque all right, but when the clerk filled in the official form to convert the pounds to pesetas I went cold. The figure he wrote down was 104.72.

'Look here,' I began to babble in my Franish, or rather in this case it was nearer Spenglish, 'the official rate for the peseta is 171.70 to the pound. I've just seen it on the board outside. What's this 104.72?'

The clerk pointed urgently to the figure and began to address me in high-speed Spanish. I didn't understand a word of it, and I felt the panic rising inside me. For the past several days I'd had a nervous eye cocked on the sinking pound, noting its downward movement against the dollar and European currency. I also knew that I'd been out of touch with affairs in Britain, but surely it hadn't sunk that low! And come to think of it, in only half an hour, too! Half an hour earlier, when I'd been converting the kids' pocket money, I'd given them a rate of 171 to the pound. What the devil had happened in England in the last 30 minutes to make it dive to 104?

The mind boggled. It couldn't have been strikes; they were nearly all on strike anyway when we left. At least, that's the way it seemed. Had there been a Communist revolution? A military coup? Had they discovered that the British Isles were sinking slowly to the bottom of the sea, undermined by all the alien drilling around its shores?

All these possibilities, wild as they may seem now, flashed through my mind as I stood at the bank counter. A man in a panic will think of anything, but in my defence I should explain that I always get nervous in banks anyway. I'm allergic to them. It's the presence of all that money that does it and I keep out of them as much as I can.

As I babbled louder, demanding explanations of what had happened to England in the last half hour, the commotion I was causing drew a small crowd of other customers around me - French, Spanish and Germans, looking at me curiously.

The Chief Fairy came in anxiously. 'What on earth's going on?' she said, pushing her way to the front.

'They're only giving me 104 pesetas to the pound! It's been cut by a third!' I said.

At this moment the bank teller leaned across the counter, tapped my arm and said, 'Look!' He'd obviously decided that the time had come to use his inadequate English, which must be an improvement on my Spanish. He turned the form towards me, pointing to the figure that had so upset me. With a heavy sigh he inked in big dots between the figures - 10.4.72.

'Ees not zee pesetas, ees zee date - ten, Haypreel, seven-two, stupido! Hokay?'

I stared at it. So it was, April the 10th! It was obviously to be my fate on this holiday to run foul of figures - on wine lists, weighing machines and now in banks. Surely this must be the end?

'You chump,' muttered the Chief Fairy.

'Okay, okay,' I muttered back, 'we can all make mistakes. You know I get nervous in places like this.' I turned to the teller who was eyeing me drily behind the counter. He shook his head slowly from side to side as though dealing with an idiot, then turned to another customer.

I felt like bawling out, 'Hokay, hokay, so it's Haypreel! And *buenas noches* to you, *senor!*' But I didn't. I tell you, in banks I'm a coward through and through. 'Sorry,' I muttered and slunk out.

15 That's Holiday Life . . .

Now that the peseta problem had been solved, the holiday began to slip by idyllically. Each day our beach platoon wound its way through the village square and must have presented a weird sight to the natives. We were loaded down with bags, rugs, beach balls, flippers, goggles, swimming togs, towels, suntan lotions, folding chairs, air beds, etc., etc., and most of it seemed to be on my back.

This was the result of the usual arguments that accompanied our daily troop movement about who should carry what. Either this item was too big or awkward for that person to carry or somebody else was already loaded down with his kite and schnorkel and couldn't possibly carry another thing. So I finished up feeling like one of those old tramps who haunt the London Embankment with all their worldly goods strapped to them.

Once on the beach in a wasp-free, fly-free zone, we'd set up camp and change into our swimming and sunbathing gear.

Some are adept at this. I am not. I think it has something to do with a total inability to stand on one leg for longer than three seconds. While trying to push the other leg into my trunks and clutching a modesty towel round me, I would totter about the beach like a drunken ballet dancer, a manoeuvre not helped by the fact that the sands would be burning the soles of my bare feet. Then it would be hotfoot - literally - over the sands to the sea.

Here the one-legged beach dance would give way to a tight-rope act as I negotiated the pebble fringe at the water's edge. Arms flailing, body swaying, feet curling, face wincing - it was an antic to frighten the fish for miles. But at last I would make the warm, welcoming waters of the Med.

We even managed to persuade the Chief Fairy to take the plunge. Normally, she can find more excuses than a cornered politician for not going into the sea, but this time she couldn't think of one. Even so, despite the comfortable temperature, she made a great production out of entering the water with clenched fists, gritted teeth and loud proclamations of 'Don't anybody *dare* splash!'

It was a pretty forlorn appeal because there was a water battle going on among the kids at the time. They were using their air beds as rival pirate ships and trying to overturn each other.

'Stop it!' she screamed as Gavin caught her with a great splashing broadside. 'Gavin, I'll kill you!'

I decided this farce of inching into warm water, goosepimple by goosepimple, had gone on long enough, so I ducked her. She spluttered to the surface, expressing herself forcefully for several seconds, then her outburst petered out as she realised how pleasant the water was. There are times when you have to be cruel to be kind, is what I always say.

That initial shock still rankled a bit though and she had her revenge when we came out of the water, dried ourselves and stretched out in the sun. I flopped onto one of the deckchairs and fell clean through it. The canvas ripped right across. It had seen a bit of service in its time and was certainly in need of replacement, but I would rather have found out some other way. I found myself pinned, bottom down, in the sand with my arms and feet flailing in the air.

My cry of anguish, which in any normal family would have brought people hurrying to my rescue, merely detonated hoots of laughter.

'Oh, quick, do get the camera!' the Chief Fairy said. 'Hurry!'

One thing it proved anyway. She wasn't the only one putting on weight. After the picture had been taken, with me locked

solid in the wooden framework, I was finally rescued, though they had the devil's own job to pull me free.

'No *paella* for you tonight,' said Amanda.

'That's what *you* think,' I said. I'd had my fill of figure problems for one holiday. This one could wait till I got home.

Throughout these days the weather remained perfect - not too hot, but just right, and the beach was quiet. In the summer the sun would blaze out of cloudless skies burning the sands so much you couldn't stand on them at all in your bare feet and you'd have to run like a mad thing to reach the sea for a swim. Then, too, there would be acres of multi-national flesh cooking in the sun and multi-lingual conversations going on under the multi-coloured beach umbrellas.

One day we counted ten different languages around us. We had a bit of a struggle identifying Norwegian, Dutch and Portuguese but the rest were fairly easy. One thing though, there was never any trouble identifying the French. They kept shaking hands with everybody. They'd even come out of the sea and start shaking hands - children included.

The only complaint we had about the weather was the wind. It came up like clockwork every day at noon and blew, sometimes fiercely, for a couple of hours before dying away again as quickly as it had sprung up. It had something to do with the climatic conditions peculiar to this configuration of coastline.

In the little Spanish square it was sheltered and you didn't notice it, but on the beach it could be a nuisance. Gavin's sombrero was for ever being whipped off his head and would go bowling across the sands until somebody leapt on it or it came to rest in another group of sunbathers. Once it raced fiercely into a picnic party and knocked a cup of steaming hot coffee out of somebody's hand. That's when Gavin heard some more languages.

To combat the wind menace every lunch time, our friend John had just bought himself a wind-breaker and one day, soon after we arrived, we tried to put it up.

It was a most complicated affair, much more complicated, it seemed to me, than a simple tent. There were five separate poles and three guy ropes for each pole - and eight of us trying to interpret the instructions. Every time we stuck a couple of pegs in the sand, the hot wind blasting across the beach would whip them out and the canvas would go billowing up like a parachute. Then we'd all leap about in a frenzy as our bare legs and bodies, already stinging from sunburn, were lashed by flying guy ropes. At this time there would be much moaning and 'ouching' going on.

'That damned thing's like a great octopus lashing us with its tentacles!' shouted Gavin, hopping about the sand clutching his wounds.

Yet it was clearly possible to erect the thing. Only a hundred yards away somebody had done it. We could see their own windbreaker fixed solidly in the sand, so I was despatched to see what the secret was.

I soon found out. 'The thing to do,' I said on my return, 'is dig a series of deep holes through the soft sand until you come to the hard stuff, then stick in each peg and cover it up. That's the trick.'

So we did, and an arduous job it was, with all that digging.

Needless to say, no sooner had we triumphantly established our wind shelter than the wind dropped and everybody moved away from it.

'It's far too hot,' said Amanda. 'Take it down.'

That's holiday life, too!

Mostly, once on the beach, all I wanted to do was stretch out, shut my eyes and think of nothing. To relax totally, to do absolutely nothing, is an art - often a neglected art on holiday. We spend so much time dashing about, seeing this, exploring that, jumping in and out of bathing gear, leaping about on the beach and doing all the things we think we ought to be doing so as not to 'waste' the holiday, that we overlook one of its greatest pleasures. The cosy ecstasy of supine inactivity.

However, with a family, wanting that blissful state is one thing - achieving it another. No sooner would I stretch out and close my eyes than urgent calls would be made to recruit me for something or other. Flippered and goggled children would shout from the waves, demanding my presence in a 'pirate' game on the air beds. Or if they'd tired of that they'd want me to dig holes, or build sand castles or search for crabs. Or ajudicate in fights and sand-throwing wars.

Wrung out by two weeks of this sort of thing, your average holiday family man returns to work and says he had a wonderful time 'just lazing on the beach.' Some lazing!

A couple of times I was shanghaied into fishing trips. I had no wish to go because I'd had experience of Gavin's fishing trips before. He likes to concentrate on the artistic side of casting the line, leaving me the messy job of cutting up the mussels and baiting the hooks. And since most of the time he lets the fish get away with the bait, I'm kept pretty busy. Indeed, only once did he ever catch a fish - ah, but what a day that was! He recalls it with wonder still.

It was the summer before when we had been fishing from a jetty near our holiday hotel in South-West Ireland. The fish were biting - two other anglers on the jetty had already pulled in several sea trout and mackerel - but Gavin had to wait a whole afternoon before he could hook one on the line. From him the fish weren't just biting, they were sitting down to eat with knives and forks, so slow was he in striking the line at the nibble.

But suddenly he shouted, 'I've got it!' He was hardly able to reel in for the sheer excitement of his very first fish. And what a fish! We stared at it in amazement as it emerged wriggling from the water. It was pure gold. I'd never seen anything like it. As it thrashed about on the end of the line its golden scales flashed in the sun.

'What is it?' he gasped. 'Is it a salmon?'

It certainly wasn't a salmon. It looked like a 3lb goldfish, but nobody on the jetty could identify it for us, so we took it back to the friendly Irish chef at our hotel. The moment he saw it he said: 'Bejasus, 'tis a very rare catch you've got there, Gavin. You could fish for 20 years and never catch another one.

This indeed is something to boast about - 'tis a golden pollock!'

'A golden pollock?' said Gavin, amazed.

'That's what it is. Now der's two t'ings you can do wit' dat fish. You can get it stuffed and mount it in a showcase on your wall at home, or you can eat it. If you want to eat it I can do you a nice fish sauce to go wit' it.'

'Oh, please,' said Gavin, 'can I have it stuffed and put it on my bedroom wall?'

The trouble was I knew very few golden pollock stuffers in this wild and empty part of Ireland. 'Well, can't we save it till we get home?' he pleaded.

'And what's it going to smell like in a fortnight's time?' I said. So we ate it. Gavin, of course, couldn't bring himself to touch a bite.

When news of his rare catch spread, somebody said to him: 'I heard you caught a golden pollock, Gavin. Are you having it stuffed?'

'Stuffed?' he said bitterly. 'That's where it's stuffed!' And he stabbed an irate finger into my midriff. It was many days before he stopped scowling at me.

Luckily, no stuffing problems arose on our fishing trips in Spain. The days slipped by happily and we didn't catch a thing.

At night we would sit under the stars in the pretty Spanish square, sipping our drinks and watching the world go by. Sometimes the hand-kissing Carlos would join us and delight the ladies. He was having an increasingly disturbing effect on the Chief Fairy. Whenever he greeted her, kissed her hand and poured out the treacle, she would go into as near a swoon as you can get without actually falling over. Romance was definitely in the holiday air - and not only for mother but for daughter, too.

Each time we entered the village square and sat at the blue tables, the young, dark-eyed Manuel hovered near us for the order, exchanging secret smiles with Christine, while we made our choices.

One night, instead of going to a village inn for dinner, we

drove to the neighbouring resort and watched a cabaret of Spanish dancers clicking their heels and castanets to throbbing guitars. It was as exciting and colourful as only Spanish dancing can be, and we were enthralled by it.

But the next day we learned that Manuel had been sad. He'd thought 'Senorita Christina' had gone away, and without saying goodbye. He was delighted to find us all back, sitting in the sun in the square at lunch-time the following day.

'*Ah, buenos dias!*' he greeted us, coming quickly to our table.

'*Buenos dias, Manuel!*' we replied. We were all becoming adept at basic Spanish phrases and Gavin even launched into '*Como esta usted?*' (How are you?)

Manuel laughed, '*Muy bien!*' (Very well) then added approvingly, 'Ees varry good! 'E speak ze Spanish!' Gavin grinned cheerfully, doffed his sombrero and said, '*Muchas gracias, senor!*' But Manuel's eyes quickly turned again to Christine while we ordered our aperitifs. We were in no doubt at all why we were the No. 1 priority at the blue chairs.

Champagne cocktails were the popular tipple at this time of day. They were so cheap - you could get a large glass for 12½p - and each day when we came up from the beach we ordered them from Manuel, with iced minerals for the children.

'Oh, I could live this life all the time,' the Chief Fairy sighed as she lay back in her chair in the sun, sipping her champagne cocktail. Dreamily, she began to hum, '*I kiss your little hand, madame . . .* ' She was off again.

'And if it hadn't been for me you wouldn't be here at all,' said Gavin. 'None of you would be here. It was my idea!'

'It was a brilliant idea,' she murmured.

He leaned forward cheekily to challenge me. 'Okay? All right? You didn't want to come, did you?'

'All right, so you had a good idea,' I conceded. 'But it's still got to be paid for, and so far it's only working out at twice the cost we estimated.'

'And who's fault is that?' he said quickly. 'Who ordered - '

'Yeah-yeah-yeah, forget it!' I interrupted.

'Oh, sure, you don't want to hear about that, do you?' he grinned.

'No, I'm tired of that tune,' I muttered.

'Never mind, it's only money, isn't it?' he went on. 'And before you say anything I've heard *you* say that! Hasn't he mum?'

'When he's enjoying himself, yes,' she murmured, her eyes still closed as she lay back in the sun.

Where, oh where, is that respectful family subservience that I've been seeking? The trouble with families is that everybody gets to know you inside out. There are no surprises.

When we rose finally to go for lunch Manuel hurried forward to assist us with our chairs - at least, that was the excuse. 'Goodbye,' he said and Christine dreamily held out her hand. He bowed to kiss it - '*Hasta la Vista!*' (Till we meet again!) he murmured.

'*Hasta la Vista!*' sighed Christine.

'Aw, isn't that nice?' said the Chief Fairy, full of champagne cocktails. '*Hasta la Vista!*' She too sighed, touching the back of her hand. She glanced round the tables for Carlos for the same treatment but he wasn't there. I was at once reminded of a bit of nonsense doggerel -

'As I was going up the stair
I met a man who wasn't there
He wasn't there again today,
I wish to God he'd go away!'

Carlos, I mean.

I took pity on her. 'Here, I'll do it for you,' I said and took her hand and kissed it.

'Aw,' she said. 'Aw!' - then threw her arms round my neck and kissed me. I don't fool myself, mind you. It's the champagne that does it. It always did.

16 Olé! It's Dad's Fandango!

Then, of course, there was the sun-bathing. Ah, yes, the sun-bathing. The first day she did her front, the second day her back and the rest of the time she turned in the sun like a roast on a spit to get her sides done. On the fifth day there was panic. 'God, I'm peeling!' she said and I was summoned urgently to the bathroom in the farmhouse to examine a minute white blob half-way down her back.

'It's a blister, isn't it?' she said anxiously, twisting round in front of the bathroom mirror. From her expression you'd have thought she'd caught the plague.

'It's about the size of a pinhead,' I said.

'Oil it quickly, darling,' she said, 'before it spreads.'

So I oiled it and it didn't spread. By this time everybody was flashing chocolate-coloured limbs around and happily showing the demarcation lines on their two-toned torsos. 'Look at that!' they'd say, or 'Yours is fantastic, how does mine look?' and 'Wait till they see this at home!'

For my own suffering I had taken on the shade of ripe khaki. But, as Alfie was asked on another occasion, what's it all about? What can a fellow *do* with an all-over tan? Sure, it's all right for my wife, now looking like a Mexican all over. Fashion being what it is, the world (at any rate, that part of the world she moves in) will see most of her tan. But what about mine? Back home it would glow beneath my trouser legs and go all the way up my back - but who would see it?

The dreary way things are ordered in the city, you can't sit in a crowded commuter train with your pin-stripes hitched above your knees and your shirt pulled back to bare your golden chest, can you? Alas, only women can win the sun-burn game - women in their summer skirts and backless and frontless dresses. Which, of course, is why they pursue the whole business with much more dedication and efficiency than men.

Study them on the beaches amid the acres of gently frying thighs and midriffs. Who glares most when you stand in their light and cast a cold shadow across a hot leg? Study their equipment - the cunning way they alternate the two-piece bikini with the low-backed one-piece swimsuit to blot out the white stripes of the bra straps.

And see how they master that strategy of exposing the maximum amount of flesh in one position - including that riveting contortion of removing the straps of a bikini top while lying face down on the sand. To the young and lissom it is a challenge to see how much they dare expose without being done - by the police, of course, not the sun.

But what happens to the men? They flop restlessly from air bed to deckchair - and sometimes through it. Their hearts are not really in the you-oil-my-back-and-I'll-oil-yours deal. It came home again to me on the third day when the Chief Fairy said to me, 'Why don't you take your sandals off and get your toes done?'

'Who's going to see my flaming sun-tanned toes?' I said. So far as I know, they haven't designed peep-toe shoes for men yet, though I agree it could happen, the way things are going. But until such male footwear comes on the market, followed quickly by mini-trousers and frontless and backless shirts, we shall continue to come second in the sun-burn stakes.

'All right, dear, don't be so testy,' she said. 'It was only a suggestion.'

We were sitting on the grass having tea in front of the farmhouse at the time, and it may be true that I was guilty of a slight testiness. Carlos had just been visiting us, doing his hand-kissing act again.

He wanted to know if we would all be his guests for dinner in town that night. The Chief Fairy said we'd love to go, and as the smiling Carlos departed with his '*Hasta la Vista!* - See you tonight!' she sighed for the umpteenth time.

'What a charming man! So elegant and slim and beautifully dressed. And such manners - oh, I do love that old-world courtesy!'

My lip curled. At that moment I was wearing a pair of baggy khaki shorts, sandals, battered sun hat and feeling far from slim after the excesses of the French and Spanish cooking. In fact, I was feeling distinctly roly-poly.

This is not the best condition for a fellow to hear his wife praise the elegance, slimness, dress and manners of somebody else. To follow it up with a suggestion that he should get his toes sun-tanned was surely turning the knife in the wound. Perhaps sub-consciously, or even consciously, she thought that I could do with a course of improvement, and where better to start than at the utmost point of my lower extremities then work upwards?

Little wonder I was short on charm that day, which is certainly something you couldn't say about Carlos.

When we met for dinner that night, at the lively little restaurant he had suggested in town, he was again oozing charm and compliments for the ladies. How well, indeed how radiant, they looked from their holiday and the sun, he said. The Chief Fairy, with two champagne cocktails inside her, lapped it up.

'Oh, do you think so?' she glittered.

'But yes! You look, how shall I say - ?' He paused.

'Oh, do say it!' she said. 'How?'

A Spanish phrase purred from his lips - I only caught the word '*bellisima*' - and she nearly swooned.

She looked down at her bare sun-tanned arms and her No. 2 cocktail dress. 'You don't think I've put on too much weight then?' Oh boy, was she fishing! But before she could haul in another load of Spanish treacle I leapt on thc line myself.

'How could he know what weight you've put on? He's only known you three days!'

'I wasn't asking you,' she retorted.

'No, no,' Carlos interjected with a devastating smile, 'I don't know what you were before, but you are just right - enchanting!'

'Oh, how nice!' she said. 'Thank you!'

'What he means,' I said, seizing her fishing line again, 'is that the Latins like their women well-stacked, too.'

She gave me a curt glance and turned back to beam at Don Juan, the treacle merchant. 'I must say I *feel* good,' she said. 'I feel absolutely marvellous, but I always do on holiday, particularly in weather like this. I'm a real sun-worshipper.' At which she demurely crossed her legs, flashing a pair of chocolate knees.

By way of retaliation I hitched up a trouser leg and flashed a sun-tanned shin of my own at one of the Spanish dancers clicking away with her castanets, but she took no notice. It wasn't the same at all. Only women, as I say, can win the sun-burn game.

However, there was no doubt my wife was right about one thing, the effect of a holiday on the personality. Away from the inhibiting forces of work, home and responsibility we become different people. Comes the holiday and that gay little fellow who has been imprisoned inside us all year long, counting the days to the jail break, finally makes it. His cell door swings open, and catch him if you can!

This is how August came to be known as the silly season. So many bright-eyed prisoners are coshing their warders and swarming over jail walls as the holiday month reaches its peak. Once free, there's no predicting what those secret personalities will do to us.

In the Chief Fairy's case her escaped personality was clearly enjoying the flattery and flirtation from this hand-kissing Spaniard. She knew there wouldn't be one waiting in the kitchen at home and she was making the most of it now.

Even the children were not immune from personality change. Christine seemed to have grown about three years older since we arrived in the village and the dark-eyed Manuel started falling in love with her. She was floating on Cloud Seven. In Gavin's case his holiday personality had merely manifested itself in more rebellion against parental authority - mainly mine - though he'd been having more than his usual quota of clashes with his sister, too. This generally occurred over helping with the tidying chores around our farmhouse apartment.

Once, out of devilment, he caught a lizard basking on the farmhouse wall outside and dropped it in front of her broom on the kitchen floor. She screamed and leapt onto a stool - though the poor thing was much more frightened of her - while Gavin fell about clutching his sides.

'That's for making me dry the dishes when I wanted to sweep up!' he said.

'You rotten beast!' she yelled at him. 'Daddy! Daddy!' As usual I was yanked in as arbiter, and in this case to chase the lizard out of the door. Gavin fled with great hoots of rebellious laughter.

Nor was I myself immune from personality change and our night at the restaurant produced a riveting example of it.

In my own case the wine and Spanish brandy certainly had something to do with it, but the metamorphosis in character after ten days of holiday was already waiting to be primed for the big leap.

I think - no, I definitely was - suffering twinges of jealousy. That was the primer. It seemed this lady-killing smoothie Carlos couldn't do anything wrong. It wasn't only his hand-kissing and silken Spanish tongue that had the Chief Fairy hypnotised, the fellow turned out to be another Fred Astaire - at least in my wife's eyes.

She accepted with alacrity when he invited her to dance. As she rose from the table, he turned to me and murmured, 'If that is all right by you?'

'Be my guest!' I said, taking another slug of brandy.

I watched them moving round the floor. He was good, very good. I took another slug of brandy. The music seemed to go on for ever, and the more it went on the more adept they became as a team, twirling about and throwing in twiddly bits that clearly delighted the Chief Fairy. I went on drinking brandy.

'Oh, that was lovely,' she breathed when they finally came off the floor. 'Thank you very much.'

He kissed her hand. In fact, he kissed both hands, which

I thought was going a bit far.

'Oh, thank you very much!' I mimicked with a mutter into my brandy, a remark that was intended only for its ears, but she heard me and gave me a cold look.

'Carlos is a beautiful dancer,' she said to the table at large.

'Isn't he though?' said Amanda, and it seemed to me that John wasn't too pleased with the idea either.

'Bully for him,' I said. 'Who wants more brandy?'

'Oh, listen!' said the Chief Fairy excitedly. 'A tango!' She turned to Carlos, who glanced at me.

'Go ahead, Twinkletoes, you've made a hit!' I said.

She swung round and glared at me.

'No, no,' said Carlos, I think genuinely concerned, 'you dance with your wife. You like the tango obviously.'

'Him!' she said. 'He couldn't tango to save his life! Come on!'

The criticism was fair. All I ever do is shuffle, as she has often reminded me, though I do try to throw in a knees bend here there where it seems to fit the music.

Again I watched them glide onto the floor and perform an efficient, if somewhat ostentatious, tango. There was a bit too much close-hugging and back-bending for my own taste. I took another slug of brandy. The prisoner personality inside me was about to leap over the jail wall. I was at this stage ticking over rather nicely, as they say, feeling a warm glow inside me - a warm glow that was demanding action.

It was the sight of one of the Spanish dancers in the cabaret that did the trick. He was drinking at the bar, having lately entertained us with a splendid display of foot-stamping and castanet-clicking.

I rose from the table and walked over to the bar as the band struck up a new number, *Granada*. 'Excuse me, *senor*, may I borrow your hat for two minutes?' I said. He smiled but before he could say yes or no, I popped it on my head - it was one of those Buster Keaton flat black things with a chin-strap - and I leapt onto the dance floor.

'*Olé!*' I shouted - or rather the escaped prisoner inside me shouted - and I launched into a finger-snapping, heel-stamping fandango. Dancers scattered - some with amazement, some I think with amusement - and gave me the floor. Head up, stiff-backed and beetling the brows in the approved manner, I stomped across the floor as the compulsive beat of *Granada* was strummed out by the band. Applause and cheers rose from the customers. They began to clap their hands to the music, which grew louder.

Tossing the head and twirling on a corner, I caught sight of the Chief Fairy, now sitting at the table. She was looking at me drily - not clapping, I noticed.

But the customers were obviously enjoying it, and in any case the mad prisoner inside me now had complete control of all my movable parts. I once did an Irish jig like this in similar circumstances and couldn't stop till the music stopped. It had nothing to do with me, you understand. As anyone who knows me will testify, it was totally alien to my character - the fellow who toils soberly and dutifully at home. It was the mad holiday fool running amok inside me.

It was the same with this one, except this time I'd had more brandy. Much more brandy. As I stomped and twirled and the cheers of the multitude grew, the faces at the table began to disappear in a blur. But still the music grew louder and faster - until, on a trumpet crescendo, I saw the room tilt sideways.

How remarkable, I thought, I seemed to be floating in space.

I *was* floating in space - but not for long. There was an almighty crash as I fell off the raised dance floor and into a potted palm. I felt no pain; it was curious, no pain at all, though I finished up on my back, tangled up with palm leaves. For several seconds everything went black, though the reason for this was quickly revealed. My hat, still hooked under my chin, was now over my face, blotting out everything.

I could hear the roars of applause as friendly hands helped me up and back to my table.

'Fantastic!' grinned John. The others were smiling, too, but not the Chief Fairy, who looked at me critically. 'Enjoy yourself?'

'Thass what we're here for,' I said, or rather slurred.

At which I flopped into my seat, resisting tumultuous calls for an encore.

But the bottle-happy buffoon inside me was by no means

finished with me yet, though my own recollections of his activities faded out at this point . . . .

17 The Moment of Truth

Next morning the little green man came for me.

It was very early and I awoke to the sound of insistent tapping. For a while I lay in a semi-comatose state with my head thumping and vaguely thinking it was part of a nightmare. Some fiendish astral blacksmith obviously had my brains spread out on his anvil and was tenderising them with his hammer. I kept my eyes closed, hoping the sound would stop but it didn't. It was real enough. It was coming from the front door of the old farmhouse, and nobody was answering it.

I've noticed before that I am invariably saddled with this chore. No one else in the family ever seems to be awakened by knockings or door bells at an early hour. They remain fast asleep, not hearing it - at least, so they claim - and I'm the one who has to climb out of the blankets to investigate.

The tapping went on and with a groan I rose. With a louder groan I fell back. All my spinal muscles seemed to be locked in a vice. Pains were shooting everywhere. As I lay panting on the bed a vague recollection of the previous night's events came back to me. It had been that backward dive into the potted palm. So much for not feeling any pain at the time. The brandy anaesthetic had worn off.

My head was throbbing, my back was aching and still the impatient caller at the farmhouse door went on tapping.

Now was as good a time as any to discover whether I would ever move again. With a superhuman effort I rolled out of the bed onto the floor and lay for a moment gathering strength to erect myself onto my hands and knees. It was agony but I set off for a slow crawl to the bedroom door.

The Chief Fairy slept on - or so she claimed - through my groaning and wailing. At the door I grabbed the doorpost and dragged myself to my feet. At least my spine was still in one piece.

I groped my way out of the bedroom and across the stone floor of the farmhouse to the source of the tapping. It stopped as I approached the glass front door.

My eyes were not focussing properly and every inch of me throbbed with aches but, my God, I wasn't prepared for what I saw! There, by the dawn light, behind the mosquito netting of the front door, was a three-foot high man with green webbed feet, bulging eyes, bulging arms, bulging chest and a single red feeler waving above his head.

I slumped into an armchair, clutching my head with a groan, 'Christ, it's that Spanish brandy!' The thing out there surely couldn't be anything else but an apparition conjured out of my alcohol-befuddled grey matter. I lay panting and vowing never to touch another drop as long as I lived.

But a moment later I was jerked out of my misery. The tapping started again. Slowly I moved towards the door and peered through the mosquito netting. I stared for several seconds before the truth dawned on me.

The little green man was my friend John's seven-year-old son, David, merely dressed up like one. He was wearing swimming trunks, cork vest, inflated arm supports, black swimming goggles, green flippers on his feet and a red Schnorkel pipe waving above his head - the complete, freckle-faced underwater man.

With a sigh of relief I opened the door. 'Hello!' he said, beaming at me behind his goggles. Half his front teeth hadn't grown down properly yet and the sight became even more gruesome, what with his red feeler waving in the air. I clutched the doorpost for support. 'Good God, David,' I said, 'I thought for a moment you were a midget Martian! You should be careful about wearing things like that at this time of day. What on earth are you doing up so early? Nobody else is awake yet.'

He wanted to know if Gavin could go with him for an early morning swim before breakfast because this was the second last day and there wasn't much of the holiday left.

'Nobody's up,' I told him. 'They're all still fast asleep.'

'Oh, all right then,' he said. 'Tell him I'll see him later.' He turned to leave, and as an afterthought I said, 'You're not going in the sea by yourself, are you?' No, his brother Jonathan was going with him. 'That's all right, as long as somebody's with you in case you sink,' I said.

'Oh, I won't sink now! I can swim! I learned yesterday.' He said it with great pride, but nevertheless still wearing his cork vest and inflated arm supports for insurance.

'Well, that's splendid - congratulations!' I said, turning to start my stagger back to bed. But he grinned excitedly at me, baring his gaps beneath his goggles. 'I knew something good was going to happen to me yesterday,' he bubbled. He's quite a little chatterbox when he gets going.

'How did you know that?'

'Because I wore my pyjamas inside out the night before. Something good always happens to you when you sleep with your pyjamas inside out!'

'It does?'

'Always!' And he went on his way, leaving me with the thought that it might not be a bad idea to wear my own pyjamas inside out in future. It might save me from the sort of nonsense I'd engaged in the disastrous night before, and for which my head and my back were now paying the price.

'How's the fandango dancer this morning then?' John greeted me cheerfully after breakfast. He and Amanda had just strolled up to the terrace of our farmhouse to see if we were ready for the beach. We were sitting in the sun.

'Fragile,' I winced, closing my eyes. This was not so much to emphasise the delicateness of my condition, it was more to shut out the sight of another little Martian who had just inflicted himself on my eyeballs. Gavin, complete with his own flippers, breathing pipe and underwater mask, sped across the terrace towards the farmhouse gate. 'See you on the beach!' he called.

'What you need is a good swim,' John sympathised, sitting down to join us.

'What I need is a good psychiatrist,' I said.

'Yes, well, swim first, then we'll get you medical help. I know just the chap in the village. Serves great champagne cocktails!'

'Yeah, I know,' I said. 'One of the blue chair doctors.'

'I must say,' smiled Amanda, 'I didn't know you could do Spanish dancing.'

'Neither did I,' I said.

There was some laughter then the Chief Fairy eyed me coolly. 'You know what else you were doing, too, don't you?'

'I've no idea and I don't want to know,' I said. I can't stand that business of having your blanks filled in for you the next day. The morning after is bad enough without somebody enlightening you about your frolics of the night before. I'd rather have a veil drawn over them for ever. But that isn't her way.

'No, I don't suppose you do,' she said, 'but I think you should at least apologise to Carlos.'

'Oh, he didn't mind,' John laughed. 'He took it in good part.'

'What - me dancing a fandango at his dinner you mean?'

'No, no, he enjoyed that. We all enjoyed that! The manager wanted to know if you were free for further engagements!'

'It wasn't then, it was later,' the Chief Fairy said. 'You were very rude to him.'

'Me?'

'Yes, you! You were drinking far too much. You kept calling him Twinkletoes and - and Don Treacle!'

'Don - Treacle?'

'Yes! God knows why! All he was trying to do was help you when you got into an argument with that bank cashier.'

Bank cashier? Oh, God! Vaguely, through the alcoholic mists a memory was stirring. I dropped my head into my hands. I remembered getting up from the restaurant table and wobbling across to the bar to return a slightly dented hat to the Spanish dancer I'd borrowed it from. I also remembered buying him a drink by way of compensation, then another face had loomed up at the bar, a face that had seemed familiar.

'Yes,' said the Chief Fairy triumphantly, 'you obviously don't remember much about that, do you? It was that bank cashier you had trouble with the day after we arrived.' She paused to let the image sink in.

'Oh God, don't bother to go on!' I muttered, but I might as well have saved my breath.

'"Ah, look who it is!" you said. "Hokay-hokay, so eet's Haypreel! And *buenos noches* to you, *senor*!" Then you threw a handful of notes on the counter and demanded that he should arm-wrestle you on the bar for what you called a pot of his crummy old pesetas.'

'Okay, leave it alone,' I said.

'I wish you had done! But no! "Come on, come on!" you said to him, "Give me your hand, you're such a big shot behind a bank counter let's see what you can do on a bar counter!"'

I couldn't remember that bit - at all. But I was now intrigued, despite myself. 'What did he do?'

'Thank God we'd left the children behind! If they'd seen you like that . . . '

'Never mind that, what did he do?'

'It wasn't what *he* did, it was what *you* did! You grabbed his arm and tried to jam his elbow on the bar. Up to that point I don't think he'd understood much of what you were saying, but he didn't like that and if Carlos hadn't rescued you in time there would have been the most terrible scene. He was going to hit you, but Carlos soothed him and brought you back to the table.'

'He did?'

'And what thanks did you give him? You held out both your hands and said "Kiss those, Twinkletoes!"'

'Oh, God, that was funny!' said John, doubling up chuckling.

'And then you started calling him Don Treacle. I was ashamed!'

She was certainly having her money's worth out of this blank-filling session and I think the same thought must have struck

Amanda, who smiled and suddenly said, 'Aw, poor Colin, it's not fair bringing it all up like that.'

'Well, if I don't tell him nobody will, and I think he should know what happens when he drinks too much,' said the Chief Fairy.

'I do believe you were a little jealous,' Amanda smiled at me.

'Me?'

'You know what they say - in *vino veritas*!'

'You'll obviously have to take up this hand-kissing lark if you want to compete there!' said John.

'No, you've got to be Spanish or French to do it properly,' said Amanda, going soft-eyed. 'They've got the knack.'

'See?' said John. 'She falls for it, too.'

'All women fall for it,' said the Chief Fairy emphatically. 'And why shouldn't we? It's a charming custom. We feel very flattered and, well, special.'

'Oh, very special, yes!' Amanda agreed.

'It's so much nicer than the curt nod you get from your average Englishman when you meet him,' the Chief Fairy added.

'That's us ruled out then!' grinned John. 'Oh, this fellow Kurt Nod will have to go! Actually, I thought he was a heel-clicking German, Koort Nod, the voman-hating schweinhund! Not one of us lovable Englishmen at all!'

'Oh, you can joke about it,' his wife said. 'But it's true.'

'Of course it is and they know it,' agreed the Chief Fairy.

'You mean we don't know how to treat women?' I said.

'Sometimes - no,' said the Chief Fairy.

'But Carlos does?'

She eyed me evenly then rose to gather up the towels and swimming things. 'It doesn't mean we fall in love with somebody just because they kiss your hands - and there's certainly no reason to call him Don Treacle. It's just a pretty compliment, that's all.'

'Yes, it is,' her ally said. 'We feel respected - and noticed.'

'My God, you should have seen the flutter he got Amanda into when we first came out here!' John said suddenly. 'We were staying at this farmhouse then and every time Amanda saw him coming up the road she'd start getting all in a tizzy, fluffing up the cushions and taking off her pinny and patting her hair!'

'Well, you can't have your hand kissed in a pinny, can you? It's just not right, is it?' Amanda protested.

'Oh, God, let's go for a swim!' said John, rising from his chair. We all got up to leave, gathering our beach things.

'Anyway,' the Chief Fairy said, 'although Amanda's right about an Englishman not being able to do it convincingly - kissing hands with grace and charm, I mean - because he's not brought up to it, he can still take a lesson from it.'

'Like what?' I said.

'Well, the lesson of the pretty compliment, and interpret it in his own way.'

'My God, these women!' I said, turning to John. 'They want their equal rights and Women's Lib, and they want compliments and hand-kissing, too!'

'Of course we do!' said Amanda, enjoying the conversation. 'Just because we're equal doesn't mean we don't enjoy men being nice to us and paying us compliments. That's the trouble, you Englishmen have stopped being chivalrous. You should try!'

There was a long silence. John and I were obviously on a losing wicket here. 'All right,' I said finally, struggling to prise a bit of chivalry from the depths of my hang-over, 'suppose we stand you a couple of champagne cocktails at lunch-time?'

'Splendid idea!' grinned John. 'Might even make it three!'

'Well, that would be very nice, of course,' said the Chief Fairy. She turned to Amanda. 'But we'd be having those anyway, wouldn't we?'

'We'd better!' said Amanda. 'Otherwise he can cook his own lunch!'

'See?' I said to John. 'We can't win!'

'No way,' he said.

'You can if you try,' said the Chief Fairy evenly.

'Okay, let's try it Italian style,' I said and pinched her bottom.

'Ouch!' she cried, and hit me with a wet towel.

Women, they're all heart.

18 A Haunting Farewell

And so we came to our last full day on the Costa Brava. The next morning we were due to return across the French-Spanish border, but this time head over the Pyrenees and up through the western provinces of France. We would have three days to reach Cherbourg.

We made the most of that last day. We were up early and swam and sunbathed and played on the beach; then at lunch-time we took up our favourite position in the blue chairs in the village square, where a downcast Manuel served us with our last lunch-time aperitifs.

It wasn't only the champagne cocktails we enjoyed here each day, it was the great Continental pastime of watching the passing parade, criticising or praising the fashions, the styles, the girls.

Some times the holiday gear would be just plain amusing. One man who entertained us vastly would stroll across the square wearing a bowler hat, shoulder length hair, ear-rings, beads and knee-length shorts!

It was difficult to tell whether he was a Red Indian tourist or a hippy holiday-maker from the City stockbroking belt.

Certainly there were times when an Englishman stood out. One I remember walked aloofly up to the brown chairs leading his family brood and seemingly unconscious of the incongruity of his fashion ensemble: deer-stalker, sports shirt, voluminous white shorts that clashed with his equally white knees and *grey socks* with his open beach sandals. All this in a temperature of 86 in the shade.

The whole passing parade always provided us with endless topics for chatter while Manuel dispensed the drinks and continued to exchange secret glances with Christine.

After lunch on that last day we made a quick run into town to buy a few final souvenirs and oranges for our journey back the next morning. The Chief Fairy also took the opportunity to weigh herself again, but the moment she stepped onto the scales she wished she hadn't. 'Oh, God, look at it!' she groaned. It had gone up another kilo. 'I'm sure those scales are wrong,' she said. 'I can't have put on that much since we arrived.'

On our way back to our farmhouse base she said that next time we came on holiday it would be a good idea to put our own bathroom scales in the car boot. I didn't think it would be a good idea at all and said so. Apart from the space problem, taking your own weighing machine on holiday strikes me as having your cake and ruining it.

Gavin groaned under his sombrero and said wearily that he hoped that was the end of the subject for the rest of the holiday because he'd had more than his fill of the discussions about his mother's weight, diets and brutal weighing machines. I agreed, so she lapsed into silence.

'And when we get back home,' he added as a parting shaft, 'I don't want you looking at my plate and telling me to eat up my food because you're on a diet again. Just because *you're* hungry doesn't mean that I am! All right?'

She said nothing, but the shaft went home.

The mention of returning to England stirred Christine from the reverie she had slipped into as we drove back to the farmhouse, 'I don't want to go back home,' she said. 'I wish we could stay here.'

'So do I,' said Gavin.

'Yes, it would be nice,' said his mother wistfully. She was thinking of all the cheap champagne cocktails and calorie-laden Spanish dishes she was going to have to give up, to say nothing of Don Treacle. Gavin was thinking of the beach and the fish-filled sea, but Christine's heart dwelt only on Manuel.

'Well, all good things must come to an end, like everything else,' I said. 'Never mind, we shall return in the summer, so that will be something to look forward to, won't it?'

But my attempt at optimism could not dispel the fact that tomorrow our Spanish frolic would be over, and for the rest of the journey back from town the family retreated silently to their own thoughts.

That night we had a farewell party. It provided the perfect end to the whole five days. After an excellent dinner at the inn we sat out under the stars with John, his family and Carlos, whom I had also invited by way of atonement. While Manuel served us for the last time Christine and Gavin, still sporting his sombrero, played for us on their guitar and melodica. Very soon we had a sing-song going. Pop songs and ballads rang out under the trees in the old Spanish square. The waiters were greatly entertained by it all, and since there were few other customers at the tables one of the brown chair waiters brought his accordian out and joined in with our blue chair orchestra. It was just the touch that the already happy atmosphere needed - a musical truce between the blue chairs and the brown chairs!

Soon the singing gave way to dancing. Manuel, emboldened by the family frolics, approached our table, bowed to me and asked if he could be permitted to dance with 'Christina'. Christine blushed delightedly. 'But of course!' I said, amused but impressed by such old-world courtesy in one so young.

At once, Carlos, to whom I had apologised for my previous excesses of party exuberance, asked me if he could also have my permission to dance with the Chief Fairy. Before I could answer, the Chief Fairy stood up and said 'Yes, please! Don't bother to ask him!' At least *that* nonsense was going to stop when we returned home.

John, grinning at this general rush for my permission, seized the moment to ask if he could dance with Amanda. I refused him and said that would be my own pleasure. He could have my permission to have the next one. 'You're too kind,' said John. 'But no hand-kissing!'

Thus the evening developed, with customers from the blue

chairs and the brown chairs joining in the music, dancing, singing and laughter till almost midnight. It was a marvellous evening. Though nobody seemed at all tired, we felt it was then time that the children were in bed. The next morning we had to be on our way.

When I made the announcement there were groans all round. Nobody wanted to leave. 'Please,' said Christine, 'just another half an hour!' We looked at her pleading face. We knew what the problem was. He was standing beside her, holding her hand. He was off-duty now. 'Tell you what,' the Chief Fairy said suddenly, 'why don't we all go back to the farmhouse and have a last cup of coffee? Manuel can come too, if he likes.'

Manuel said he would love to. So did John and Amanda. As for Carlos he said he would be charmed and kissed her hand again. 'Oh, that settles it!' she laughed.

After all the fun of the party, a last coffee in the farmhouse was just what we needed to decelerate our emotions to the low-gear mood for sleep.

Gradually the excitement and chatter subsided, and people began to yawn in armchairs. Whether it was because we let the mood slip too low or whether it was the candle-lit atmosphere of the old farmhouse, I don't know, but we finished up the night frightening the wits out of everybody with ghost stories. The kids loved them, of course, and kept huddling closer and asking for more. Looking back now, I think what started it was the Chief Fairy recounting the fright she had had with the cackling bubbly-jock in Brittany. Everybody laughed.

'But I'd never heard one before, I'd no idea what it was!' protested the Chief Fairy. 'Anyway,' she turned to me, 'I can remember a time when you weren't so brave. What about that time in Hampshire?'

'What time in Hampshire?'

'You know very well. That ghost in the bedroom, tell them about that!'

I hesitated. The tale was not particularly to my credit.

'Oh, yes!' said Gavin. 'Tell us about that.'

'No, it's time you were all in bed,' I said.

'No, please!' said Gavin, huddling closer to his mother.

'Tell us about the ghost in the bedroom! Go on, please!'

I glanced round the group. Their eyes were on me and their interest aroused. I could see that I would have to tell it - so I did.

It happened one night while the Chief Fairy and I were spending a weekend in a 16th-century Hampshire pub, a low, two-storey, rambling place of oak beams, timbered passages and leaded windows. In our room were two single bedsteads, which was a bit of a blow because we're believers in the warmth and comfort of a double bed.

In the early hours of the morning I awoke suddenly, vaguely aware that something had aroused me, some presence. The room was dark and silent, yet it seemed a vibrating silence left by an earlier disturbance. Without looking I realised that my wife was awake in her own bed.

'What was that noise?' she whispered.

Here I may say that if it's true - and I'm sure it is - that any wife knows her husband better than he knows himself, it is because marriage constantly throws up great chances for her to plunge the dipstick into his character. Such a moment is this, when things go bump or whir in the night.

Prodded awake by a nervous wife hissing, 'What's that noise?' one man will leap from his bed and charge down to tackle the suspected intruder. Another will stop at the top of the stairs and call, 'Who's that down there?' in the secret hope that whoever it is will flee for his life. At a lower level of sludge on the character dipstick there is the fellow who, equally alarmed, will say to his wife, 'My God, you'd better go and have a look!' Which, I suppose, shows us where sex equality and the age of the anti-hero have got us. But I was not to be recognised at any of these levels.

'What noise?' I said. 'I can't hear any noise,' and made to pull the blankets over my head.

Before I could do so, however, it came again, a strange, whirring, moaning sound. 'There it is again!' she gasped in the darkness.

'It's only the wind in the chimney,' I said.

There was silence for a moment. In the dark she was obviously working something out, then came another urgent whisper: '*There is no chimney!*'

In the dark I was working something out. She was right. 'It's the wind in the eaves,' I said.

'Look out of the window,' she said.

Almost immediately outside the room was a sycamore tree and it was as still as though it had been painted on the night sky. Not a breath of wind stirred.

'I think I'll come into your bed,' she said.

'Don't be ridiculous,' I said. 'There's probably a perfectly reasonable explanation.' And then it came again, unmistakably the sound of wind whirring in the corner of the windless room. 'All right, come on in if you want to,' I muttered quickly. My trouble is that I've read too much Dennis Wheatley.

When she finally finished clawing her way into my bed we lay awake for nearly an hour, but the sound didn't come again. And yet there was still the sense of some presence in the corner of the darkened room, as though we were being watched, silently. Then, quite suddenly, it departed - that is, the sensation of being watched disappeared and the room was back to normal.

Next morning I mentioned the incident to the landlord as we were having breakfast. He looked at me curiously, then said it was probably the wind. But I knew that sycamore tree hadn't lied.

'Why, you don't think we're haunted, do you?' he said and forced a little smile. I had a strong feeling it was not the first time he'd heard about it.

'Good Lord, no, I don't believe in ghosts,' I said casually.

'But you were pretty damned anxious for me to jump into your bed,' said the Chief Fairy.

'Nonsense. You wanted to come in so I let you.'

'Oh, sure!' she grinned. She knew all right. I'd failed the dipstick test.

To this day I still don't know what that strange, whirring moan was that rose in the corner of our bedroom, though the Chief Fairy was convinced it was a poltergeist. For his own reasons - perhaps because of the possible effect on his customers - the landlord wasn't saying. But I was positive he knew something.

The tale, which was listened to by our farmhouse guests, at first with amusement then awe, started a flood of personal creepy experiences in the haunting world. For half an hour or so the children grew bigger-eyed and huddled closer, yet still demanded more scares.

But at last, after one particularly horrific tale of a recurring nightmare about an evil tree that guarded a lonely country road and stretched out its branches towards those who passed by it at dusk, Amanda shivered and said it was time they all went home.

It was a strange note on which to finish an evening of such merriment.

At the farmhouse door we said our goodnights and goodbyes and hoped that we'd all see each other again in the summer. Manuel bid a tender goodnight to 'Christina' and Carlos bowed to his last hand-kissing trick with the Chief Fairy, but I had a feeling that his mind wasn't entirely on it. I noticed that as he stepped out into the darkness of the farmhouse drive, past the old, gnarled tree that stood like a sentinel at the gate, he kept close to the other departing guests. In fact, they all kept tightly together . . . .

19 Hello, Cat! Hello, Loo!

Inevitably a sense of anti-climax set in as we drove off the next morning on our return journey. For many miles we travelled in silence, each alone with his or her own thoughts and memories of the holiday we had had. The hour itself also had something to do with our low-key mood, for we had set off early to make as much distance as possible before the day was out.

Yet it would be unfair to the Pyrenees and the route we took through them to describe the journey itself as an anti-climax. The scenic splendours were breathtaking.

By mid-afternoon we had left the coastal plain and were travelling through mountain passes where pine forests soared up on each side towards snow-capped peaks, and mountain rivers tumbled by the roadside and skirted colourful little villages. It was not the sort of setting in which the spirits could remain low for long, and soon the car was once again filled with excited chatter. Twice we stopped to take pictures and a third time for our daily picnic.

We made good time that day and by dusk were able to put up in a village inn among the vineyards of Armagnac in South-West France. Once again Gavin made his customary inquiry while I booked the family room, '*Où se trouve la toilette, s'il vous plaît?*' We had been well served in this department while in Spain, but his old suspicion had now returned. However, he was pleased to find this village inn was also well equipped.

The next morning, after our croissants and coffee, we were

on our way early, heading north towards Bordeaux. We stopped only once. It was at a roadside stall among the vineyards where we bought a speciality of the area, a jar of *pruneaux d'Armagnac*, which are prunes steeped in liqueur. We had tasted them at the village inn and thought them delicious. However, since they were prunes and we still had a long way to go through unknown loo territory, we decided to keep the jar till we got home.

From Bordeaux, a city of unexpected beauty and the centre of the region's wine industry, we pressed on north through the Atlantic resort of La Rochelle, Nantes, Rennes and by nightfall had reached our little family hotel in Dinard once again. This was our last overnight stop.

The kids were delighted to be back in Dinard and after dinner headed straight along the sea-front to the Dodgems, Gavin for the fun of the ride, Christine for the flirting fun of the riders.

Not for the first time I thought how resilient children are. What seemed pangs of unendurable agony because of our departure from the pleasures of Spain, the beach, the village square and Manuel, suddenly disappear like a morning mist when a new excitement looms. Perhaps it's just as well.

Looking back on all that had happened, the 2,000-mile journey, the nights we had spent in strange places, the crisis over the £20 wine bill, the tent disaster and all the other things we'd been involved in since we set out from home, it seemed as though we had been away two months, not two weeks. This, I suppose, is another bonus of the touring holiday.

The next day we boarded the ferry at Cherbourg and, in contrast to our outward journey, we had a smooth crossing to Southampton on a fine spring day.

Back home, amid much excitement, we collected Smokey from her cats' hotel and were greeted with loud miaowing - which could have been complaints or pleasure at our return. But I'm afraid I wouldn't know.

Happily, the house was still standing, the burglars hadn't called and, well, it was rather nice to be back, too. We got out the glasses for a celebration drink to our safe return and to the whole inspiration of Gavin's holiday essay.

'We could have those prunes in liqueur, couldn't we?' said the Chief Fairy brightly.

'Just the job,' I said. 'Let's pour 'em out.'

We were quite safe with prunes now we were back home to our own loos.